W9-CRT-868

SEGO LILY

©PAT O'HARA

GRAND CANYON COUNTRY

Its Majesty and Its Lore

By Seymour L. Fishbein

Prepared by the Book Division
National Geographic Society, Washington, D. C.

FREYA CASTLE FROM CAPE FINAL ON THE NORTH RIM; PRECEDING PAGES: SUNSET FROM NEAR HOPI POINT ON THE SOUTH RIM

JEFF GNASS; TOM BEAN (PRECEDING PAGES)

REDBUD AND MAIDENHAIR FERNS AT DEER CREEK NARROWS

COBY JORDAN

GRAND CANYON COUNTRY:
Its Majesty and Its Lore

By Seymour L. Fishbein

Contributing Photographers: Tom Bean,
David Hiser, Danny Lehman

Published by
The National Geographic Society
Gilbert M. Grosvenor,
President and Chairman of the Board
Owen R. Anderson,
Executive Vice President
Robert L. Breeden,
*Executive Adviser to the President
for Publications and Educational Media*

Prepared by
The Book Division
William R. Gray, *Director*
Margery G. Dunn, *Senior Editor*

Staff for this Special Publication
Toni Eugene, *Managing Editor*
Thomas B. Powell III, *Illustrations Editor*
Marianne R. Koszorus, *Art Director*
Victoria D. Garrett, Bonnie S. Lawrence,
Researchers
Barbara Bricks, *Contributing Researcher*
Richard M. Crum, Tom Melham, Jennifer
C. Urquhart, *Picture Legend Writers*
Sandra F. Lotterman, *Editorial Assistant*
Artemis S. Lampathakis, *Illustrations Assistant*

Engraving, Printing, and Product Manufacture
George V. White, *Director,*
John T. Dunn, *Associate Director,* and
Vincent P. Ryan, *Manager,
Manufacturing and Quality Management*
Lewis R. Bassford,
Production Project Manager
Heather Guwang, Richard S. Wain,
Production
R. Gary Colbert, Elizabeth G. Jevons, Lisa L.
LaFuria, Teresita Cóquia Sison, Dru M.
Stancampiano, Marilyn J. Williams,
Staff Assistants

Bryan K. Knedler, *Indexer*

Copyright © 1991 National Geographic Society.
All rights reserved. Reproduction of the whole or any part of the
contents without written permission is prohibited.
Library of Congress CIP Data: page 199

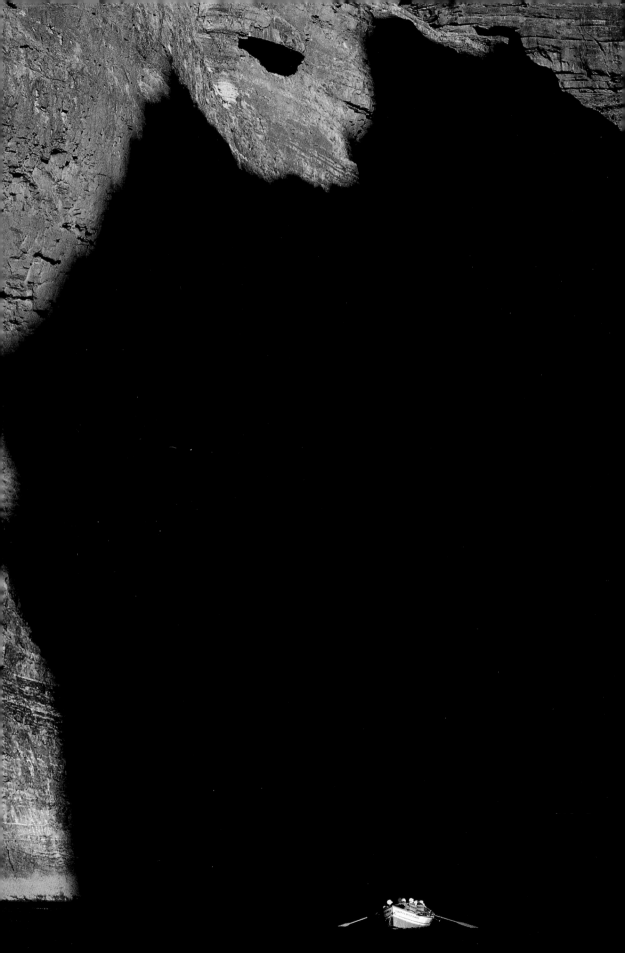

Contents

ALUMINUM DORY IN MARBLE CANYON

DUGALD BREMNER

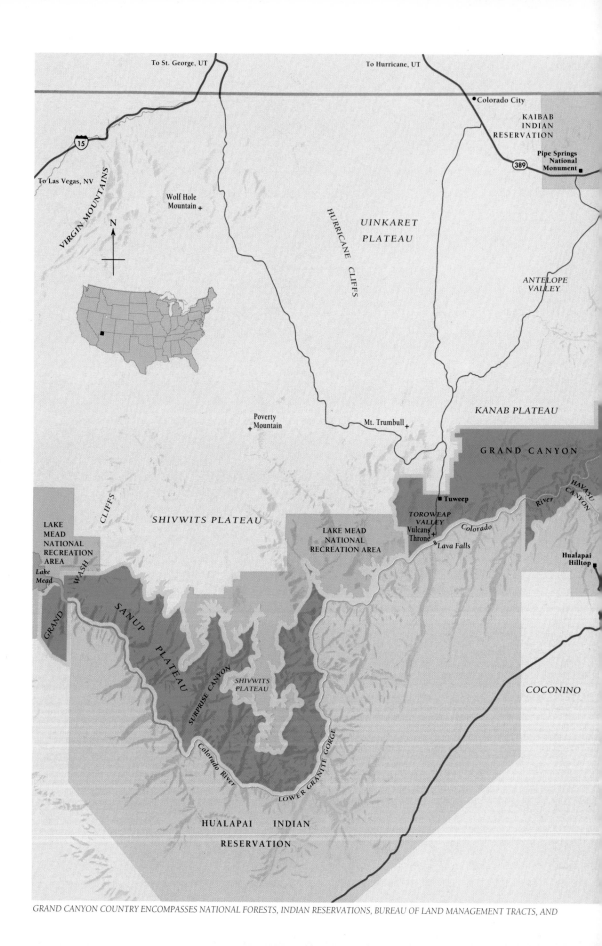

GRAND CANYON COUNTRY ENCOMPASSES NATIONAL FORESTS, INDIAN RESERVATIONS, BUREAU OF LAND MANAGEMENT TRACTS, AND

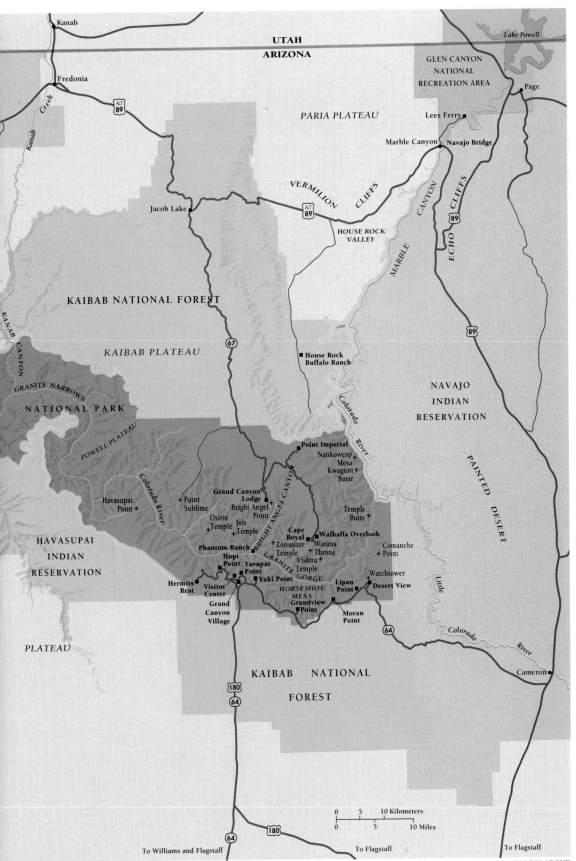

NATIONAL RECREATION AREAS; IT EXTENDS FAR BEYOND THE BOUNDARIES OF THE NATIONAL PARK, HIGHLIGHTED IN YELLOW ABOVE.

JOHN K. HILLERS / COURTESY SMITHSONIAN INSTITUTION

Canyon Country

An Introduction

Could this be Arizona, deep in the Sunbelt, the state with a giant saguaro on its license plate? One morning in March a balding man of middle years, lightly clad, ventures out of the venerable El Tovar Hotel. Snowflakes melt on his pink pate and bleed down his cheeks, about the way tears do. He grimaces, grumbles a bit, shakes his head. "I left Ohio for this?"

Less than a mile straight down from where the snowbird shivers, there's not a hint of snow. Just another 70-degree day amid cottonwoods and willows and cactuses all in green, surrounded by rock walls that rise a mile or more, roofed by thick cloud. This is Arizona, the Grand Canyon State.

Overnight the skies clear, and from the instant of daybreak on the South Rim of Grand Canyon National Park a man knows why he left Ohio. Or Japan, or England, or Finland, or Germany, or Australia. For this: A gash in the earth beyond imagining, from 600 feet to 18 miles across, reaching down from cool, piny plateaus to scorching desert, exposing nearly two billion years of earth's history, preserving shelters and shrines and storehouses and the arts and crafts of Native Americans who have found a home here for at least 4,000 years. Some still call it home.

The canyon sweeps in ragged loops from near the Utah border south and west for 277 miles to the Nevada border. In all that distance only a single dirt road penetrates to its deepest depths—but does not reach across. There is an old turn of phrase in canyon country, reported by historian Juanita Brooks: "What God hath put asunder, let no man join together." Except for the two-lane span across the narrow northern neck of the canyon, the plateaus abutting the gorge remain asunder. *(Continued on page 18)*

Pioneer voyager through the Grand Canyon,
Maj. John Wesley Powell confers in 1871
with Tau-gu, a Paiute. The one-armed Civil
War veteran led two river trips through
the gorge, aiming, he said, "to add a mite
to the great sum of human knowledge."

13

14

MICHAEL COLLIER

KOLB BROTHERS

W*ith "a crash . . . the boards broke like egg-shells," noted Emery Kolb of a boat-splintering upset on the wild waters of the Colorado in the winter of 1911. Safe ashore, Emery pokes his head through the stove-in* Edith *before he and his brother, Ellsworth, begin repairs. The Kolb brothers ran the Colorado to film and photograph the wonders of the canyon. Rapids still batter river runners' dories (opposite).*

15

Winter light reaches the Colorado in late morning near Elves Chasm. Boats of a 1990 photographic expedition recall voyages made in 1889–1890 to survey for a proposed water-level railroad through the canyon. One trip ended with the loss of three lives. Photographs taken on a second run (opposite), compared with today's prints, help document changes in canyon ecology and geologic features.

RALPH LEE HOPKINS

ROBERT BREWSTER STANTON, COURTESY OF THE NATIONAL ARCHIVES

Out of those canyon depths rise peaks in tantalizing hues, brilliant or somber, transformed in a moment's shifting play of sun and cloud upon the patina of rock. Science and art discovered this landscape in the 19th century, when the questing spirit and the romantic imagination soared. Clarence Dutton, career soldier, adventurer, and geologist, began a tradition of naming these landmark buttes temples and thrones and castles. The tradition endured; few of the heights are called mountains; yet some stand taller than any mountain east of the Rockies. And we look down on them.

Dutton, the most inspired of all the votaries who have ever tried to paint these wonders in words, penned a now classic description of "the most sublime and awe-inspiring spectacle in the world." He noted that "Grand Cañon" had been applied to chasms cut by the Yellowstone River in Wyoming and the Arkansas in Colorado. "Flagrant piracy," he fumed; those picturesque "river valleys" are as like to the Grand Canyon as the Alleghenies are to the Himalaya.

Cataracts gush out of canyon walls; the life-giving water, so precious here, makes the sere desert cliffs bloom with lush drapery, green and florid. The waters of other streams run milk-blue over creamy pastel beds and dams of travertine, an astounding sight even with foreknowledge from the guidebooks. Travelers who come upon these waters feel as if they had suddenly been transported to tropic seas and coral isles.

Rock layers here teem with relics of living things—seashells, reptiles that roamed ancient deserts, amphibians that roamed ancient shores. In the canyon scientists have discovered the fossil wing prints of insects, the footsteps of lizards, the tracery of wind upon sand dunes, the ripples of currents that flowed and the patter of raindrops that fell hundreds of millions of years ago, before any mammal walked the earth, before any dinosaur.

Far down in the canyon runs one course of dark, red-brown rock that formed 550 million years ago in a seabed aswarm with trilobites. At one famous site salt leaches out of the rock. For centuries Hopi Indians have made ritual pilgrimages to the place, trekking more than a hundred miles from their mesa villages to the east, across the desert and down steep, toilsome canyon paths to gather the salt for food and for sacred ceremony.

Indians mined clay stone here, too, mixing it with deer tallow to make a bright red cosmetic that also protected them from cold and the desert sun. Bits of reddish copper ore attracted prehistoric craftsmen, and in the 19th century white prospectors moved in to mine copper, silver, lead, and asbestos. Gold, prized by all, lies all through the river sands—but in such infinitesimal quantities that no one ever made it pay. As late as the 1960s the richest uranium mine in the nation operated hard by Maricopa Point, a popular vantage for South Rim sightseers. The skeleton of the mine works still stands, a reminder of canyon history and something of an eyesore as well. Far to the west another tower rises on the canyon rim, with loose sheet metal clanking in the wind—the remains of a bat-guano mine, a costly venture that lasted but a few years in the late 1950s.

The prospect of gold—the legendary Seven Golden Cities of Cibola—lured the first white men to Grand Canyon country. The conquistador Francisco Vásquez de Coronado, persisting in a fool's errand, sent a detachment of soldiers. In September 1540 they reached the South Rim. Just where is not known, but their description of the scene suggests the eastern reaches of today's national park, between Moran Point and Desert View. Hopi Indians had guided the Spanish soldiers to a view of the river, but would not reveal the trails that led down to it. The Spaniards poked about in a futile search for a way through what a later Spanish traveler called a "calaboose of cliffs and cañons." Three of them ventured about a third of the way down, then gave it up, discovering a great truth: ". . . what seemed to be easy from above was not so, but instead very hard and difficult." Hundreds of thousands of tenderfoot canyon hikers rediscover that truth every year, despite lectures and pamphlets and cautionary signposts. I wheezed and wobbled and sweated with quite a few other rediscoverers in the course of my wanderings.

Cibola eluded the Spaniards. They came too soon. Cibola lives today, about a hundred road miles beyond the western bounds of the canyon, luring throngs with glitter and titillation and the prospect of gold. Some drawn to it also find their way to the canyon. A steady stream of traffic flows back and forth between the stark splendor of the gorge and the golden glitter of Las Vegas.

After the first Spanish explorers retreated, more than two centuries passed before another white man recorded a visit to the canyon. This was Franciscan missionary Francisco Tomás Garcés, who in the summer of 1776 came upon a "deep passage . . . steep-sided like a man-made trough." Through it coursed a tawny stream, which he called *Río Colorado*—Red River.

Without knowing its recent history, anyone looking at the Colorado today might think the good padre color-blind or loco. No. Others have seen what Father Garcés saw, but today's Colorado, often green, is no longer the river he saw. It is no longer the muddy river that pounded and exhilarated Maj. John Wesley Powell through two pioneering voyages down the Grand Canyon in 1869 and 1872, voyages that drew from him a supreme tale of adventure, scientific discovery, and descriptive narrative.

It is not the river President Theodore Roosevelt saw in 1903, when he first encountered the canyon, "the most impressive piece of scenery I have ever looked at. . . . It is beautiful and terrible and unearthly." He wanted it preserved without a "building of any kind, not a summer cottage, a hotel, or anything else, to mar the wonderful grandeur, the sublimity, the great loveliness and beauty of the Canyon. Leave it as it is. You cannot improve on it." I first read these words in a South Rim hotel, amid a cluster that had begun to sprout even as Roosevelt sounded his plea.

When Roosevelt described the canyon, it was known as Grand Canyon Forest Reserve; he proclaimed that land the Grand Canyon Game Reserve in 1906. Despite good intentions, the reserve, which protected game animals but excluded predators from that protection, in time produced an ecological fiasco. An ardent conservationist, Roosevelt in 1908 created Grand Canyon National Monument, forerunner of the national park. As a godfather of the reclamation movement, Teddy Roosevelt helped bring forth the federal dam-building era that made the river what it is today—what author Philip Fradkin called "the most used, the most dramatic, and the most highly litigated and politicized river in the country, if not the world."

In the Grand Canyon the Colorado remains a river of power, demanding skill and respect from those who attempt to maneuver through it. The river runners I observed, some with decades of experience, were ever in awe of it, never took it for granted. Yet for all its power, it is a push-button river, turned on and off by the hand of man. Glen Canyon Dam, just beyond the head of the canyon, has radically changed the river's vital signs—its pulse, its temperature, its pallor. Scientists have spent years and millions of dollars studying the changes, measuring benefit and loss in the canyon environment; they will continue to study them. In some respects the unnatural river has enriched the life along its banks. Seasonal floods no longer scour the riverbanks, and exotic streamside vegetation has flourished. Exotic fish life has taken hold. In an ironic twist, the plants and fish are sustaining endangered species and nurturing others threatened by loss of habitat elsewhere. But native fish species have vanished; erosion has diminished riverside beaches and threatened the stability of prehistoric settlements built on the river terraces. Whatever the river has lost or gained, it is not the river nature ordained, but instead a harnessed stream fed through the grandest of canyons and a national park on a timetable set by peak demands for electrical energy.

The canyon extends far beyond the bounds of the national park, even with a major park extension in the mid-1970s that incorporated Marble Canyon and Grand Canyon National Monuments and part of the Kaibab National Forest. On the southern side of the gorge only about 100 of the 277 miles of canyon wall lie within the park; Indian reservations claim the rest, though the boundaries are in lingering dispute. On the north side—that chunk of Arizona sundered from the rest of the state by the canyon—canyon country beyond park boundaries encompasses a detached fragment of the Lake Mead National Recreation Area and other public lands administered by the U.S. Forest Service and the Bureau of Land Management, all within the 8,400 dry and mostly empty square miles of the storied Arizona Strip.

Some four million people visit the park each year, most of them day-trippers crowding the splendid viewpoints on the South Rim, savoring the big picture from different angles through changing aspects. I joined them often, watching the canyon awake and catch fire at dawn, doze under a veil of midday haze, flare up again with the westering sun, and flame out at nightfall. But this glorious cycle takes the better part of a day, longer than most visitors stay. I saw them come and go, filled with wonder, sometimes saddened by the press of a short stay. I saw an elderly woman who had alighted from a tour bus at the South

Rim Visitor Center, where she lingered among the striking displays and the racks of books and maps and pictures. Before long the driver called out, "We load in 20 minutes." The canyon rim lies a quarter of a mile away, and the anxious woman, clutching her cane, hurried off for a glimpse of it.

"To truly experience the Grand Canyon," says Park Superintendent Jack Davis, "people ought to have the opportunity to spend a night at the rim, with sunrise and sunset, to enrich the evening at one of the interpretive programs. Most people don't spend the time needed to really see the park. They come just for the day." In the busy summer months roads and parking lots are packed; 20,000 tourists a day visit. The growing influx of visitors places further demands on already strained facilities. There may come a time when the park can no longer hold all the people who come. On the river and in the more popular areas of the backcountry, that time arrived years ago; permits from the National Park Service are required.

I remember a chill day in December, dry and crisp as new money, when a couple of guys and their dolls flew in from Vegas. They picked up some wheels at the airport near the South Rim and set out to do the park. They pulled up at Yavapai Point, strolled around the museum, took in the nice view out across the canyon, then tagged behind a uniformed college boy, a volunteer giving a spiel about the plants and animals on the South Rim. He pointed to some jays, flitting about and squawking, and told how they lived on the nuts from the pine trees. The visitors smiled at the tale of the jaybirds. As they strolled, one kept clenching and unclenching a fist. "You know," he told his friend, "I don't feel right without a pair of dice in my hand." Soon they glanced at their watches. Time for lunch and the curio shops, then maybe a few more stops to look at the pretty rocks before the short hop back to Cibola, where the real action is.

I found the real action here—here on the South Rim along the viewpoints and on the grinding trails in the unforgiving backcountry below the rim; in canyon country beyond the park, east to the edge of the Painted Desert and the rutted brushlands dotted by Navajo hogans, and far to the west where Hualapai cowboys ride and the Colorado River widens into Lake Mead. I found it crossing the canyon, down through the eons until the trough bottoms out, and slowly up the other side, where the miles grow longer and the rest stops more frequent. I found it on the cool North Rim, where the snows lie deep and the ponderosas stand tall; at the lonely park promontory that inspired the classic word picture of the canyon; on a remote brink where people crawl on their bellies for a look down the dizzying walls coated with frozen lava; on horseback through baking valleys under bright red cliffs, where buffalo roam and Mormon cowboys drift their cattle over deadbeat sagebrush range. Finally, I found it down the great river in dories, through glassy waters and gentle riffles, twisting eddies and explosive waves, their roar funneled by the soaring walls. Louder and louder. A sobering sound. Welcome to the grand canyon-cutter. Real action. It took more than a day.

KAIBAB LIMESTONE FROM POINT IMPERIAL

GREG PROBST

HIKERS DESCENDING THE SOUTH KAIBAB TRAIL

TOM BEAN

BUCKSKIN GULCH, PARIA CANYON – VERMILION CLIFFS WILDERNESS AREA

©LARRY ULRICH (BOTH)

26

KAIBAB LIMESTONE, ASPENS, AND BRACKEN FERNS ON THE KAIBAB PLATEAU

O'NEILL BUTTE AT SUNRISE FROM YAKI POINT

GARY LADD

South Rim Country

*A*ugust shower descends at sunset in the Grand
Canyon's ageless drama, water against stone.
Shadows cloak the South Rim near Yavapai Point.

WILLARD CLAY; GARY LADD (PRECEDING PAGES)

Spring snow drapes a solitary piñon pine at Mohave Point. Beyond it, clouds ring 6,613-foot-high Osiris Temple, named for the Egyptian god of the underworld.

B ack home one evening, between journeys to canyon country, I attended a performance of *The Tempest*. Shakespeare productions, regrettably, are sometimes unmemorable. His words, never. The expansive vision of the play's Prospero spun me westward faster than any jet could, to the "cloud-capp'd towers, the gorgeous palaces, the solemn temples."

Soon I was back among them, the congealed oceans and deserts and deltas and swamps, layer upon layer of rock slashed by earth movement, carved by wind and water into mesas and buttes and alcoves and terraces, fancied into sacred monuments to far-flung deities—an ecumenical trough of shrines trading colors with sky and cloud.

On the South Rim of Grand Canyon National Park the stream of devotees may slow at times, but it never stops, even in the dead of winter, 6,860 feet above sea level. At Yaki Point and Hopi Point along the road that threads the rim—choice sites for watching the canyon awake—motors are purring in pitch dark, and bundled figures silently wait in cars and vans. With first light the early birds slowly emerge into the subfreezing air, shivering children trying to make their heads disappear into coat collars.

A blue haze bathes the dim canyon depths as light encroaches on the eastern barrier known as the Palisades of the Desert. Clouds take on color, blue trimmed with pink, and so do the canyon walls in the brightening twilight—dark red tones in the middle rock layers known as Hermit shale and the Supai formation of sandstones and shales. They are rich in iron oxides, and the pigment seeps down below them to stain the hard, steep, unmistakable layer called Redwall limestone, though its red is only skin deep. Beneath the bright patina, the rock is light gray.

Finally the sun—and across the canyon on the North Rim, the eastward facing panels of the rimrock layer, the famous Kaibab limestone upon which we also stand, begin to glow like distant billboards. Sunrays stab down in, and, strangely, shadows lengthen: rhythm of light and shade through tucks and swales and ridges.

Below the ridges beside us thermals rise, and on them ravens soar, playing the currents. Free riders. I can scarcely see a wing beat.

Window on geology, Yavapai Point offers South Rim visitors a sweeping vista of vertical walls, shrubby terraces, and deep gorges. Vishnu Temple rises in silhouette on the horizon. Stepped layers give O'Neill Butte, at far right, its distinctive profile.

TOM BEAN

At Hopi Point 11-year-old Anna Jeffery, droopy with jet lag and hunger and cold, asks, "How long are we going to stay here?"

"Till the sun gets to the bottom of the canyon," replies her father, Ross Jeffery. "Maybe it never gets there," Anna breaks it off, defeated. Maybe Anna knows something. Preparing for the visit, she has done some reading, back home in a suburb of Sydney, Australia.

"The birthplace of monuments the beginning of temples. . . . GRAND CANYON made by the liquid snake. . . . a gorge so deep the sky is narrow as a line of blue thread."

On the vertical it is nearly a mile down to the bottom. Poet Philip Wofford heard "the sound of time working here in the birthplace of monuments the beginning of temples . . . . GRAND CANYON made by the liquid snake. . . ." It is "a gorge so deep," he wrote, that "the sky is narrow as a line of blue thread."

Hopi Point is a good place to see the liquid snake; here it courses through some formidable snake pits—Horn Creek Rapids and Granite and Hermit, and on downstream, notorious Crystal Rapids. West of Hopi, at Pima Point overlook, you may see the thrashing of Granite. Still, at this distance, there is no bite or fright in the Colorado. You can only see what the river and its great crosshatch of tributaries have done to earth's crusty shell here, and can only sense its power. The rapids are but names on a map. River runners know better and, later, running with them, a passive witness through the pounding froth, so would I.

On the promontory that includes Hopi Point stands a memorial to the pioneer river runner, the inspiration of all who follow—Maj. John Wesley Powell, "the Major," veteran of the Civil War that took his right arm, professor of geology, student of paleontology and ethnology, explorer of the tumultuous artery of the Southwest.

Within view of that monument to Powell and his gritty band of scientists and adventurers stands another memorial, of sorts, recalling the repeated—and mostly futile—attempts to mine riches from the canyon. This is the abandoned tower of the Lost Orphan Mine. It began in the 1890s as a copper mine and, like others in the harsh desert terrain, eventually found hauling tourists a richer prospect than digging and hauling ore. But with the coming of the Atomic Age in mid-century, the Lost Orphan began to pay off. It was located in a particular mineral formation — breccia pipe — that often indicates the presence of uranium. The Lost Orphan became one of the richest uranium mines in the land, noisome and unsightly on the brink of a matchless landscape, but producing more than four million pounds of uranium, as well as nearly seven million pounds of copper and 107,000 ounces of silver.

Mining has ended in the national park, but canyon country is rich in breccia pipes, and uranium mining remains a sore point on other sites, Indian land and public land, some on ground held sacred in Native American tradition. On the lonely Arizona Strip north of the canyon, says Dan Dagget of the Sierra Club, public lands are "littered" with uranium claims. Low prices have kept a lid on activity, but if the claims are pursued and mining develops, Dagget envisions new highways and roaring ore trucks across "one of the wildest places left in the Southwest."

And at Maricopa Point near the Powell Memorial, above the pyramids and temples and the liquid snake, the Lost Orphan's tower still stands, something of an eyesore; park officials estimate it would take more than 300,000 hard-to-find dollars to remove the mine works.

A sturdy new rail fence at Maricopa, shunting visitors away from once well-trodden paths, marks a small victory for conservation over extinction. Within the fenced precincts dwells the only known population of sentry milk-vetches. The total population numbers less than 500 plants, dull, nondescript little mats rooted in crevices of the Kaibab limestone — a hard living at best, made much harder by the footfalls of visitors. The park was reluctant to close off the popular walk, but the U.S. Fish and Wildlife Service made known its intent to list the plant as an endangered species — hence the fence. Now the sentry milk-vetch clings to its rocky roothold without the hazard of mass trampling. It is classified in a family that includes poisonous locoweed, but the nontoxic milk-vetches won a reputation in the Old World for increasing the milk output of goats.

A sturdy pipe fence hems the rim at Mather Point to shield our species from danger, a tumble down the verge, perhaps a few feet to some talus or brush, or perhaps much farther. For many, driving in from the park's south entrance, this is the first stop, the first glimpse of the Grand Canyon, its beauty and its immense plunge. There are those for whom no pipe railing can keep stomach and knees from stiffening. One day a couple approached from the parking lot, he in a semicrouch with video gear — producer, cinematographer, auteur — panning the yawning gorge. Shadows curved around the alcoves in the Redwall limestone. The Coconino sandstone, third layer from the top, was a gleaming band below the North Rim opposite. The eastern canyon dozed in a somber haze. The filmmaker's spouse followed behind him; then, as she neared the rail and sensed the void beyond, she broke stride and turned back. "I'll watch it at home," she said, to no one in particular.

On a waning winter day I find myself at Yavapai, another fine South Rim viewpoint, with a museum that sets forth the natural history of the canyon and helps us sort out the welter of shrines. Kindled by Ra's declining rays, the temples flare, from their Redwall limestone bases, up steps and slopes of sandstone and shale, to the tough sandstone crowns. They glow first to the north—Isis, Buddha, Manu—gradually across the wavy cleft of Bright Angel, a major side canyon, to Deva, Brahma, Zoroaster. The gods summon us to vespers. Then slowly Ra departs. The shadows splay, shrouding the depths and the parapets and the buttresses and towers, until all is darkness.

The gods summon us to vespers. Then slowly Ra departs. The shadows splay, shrouding the depths and the parapets and the buttresses and towers, until all is darkness.

The temples once were part of the main plateau. As the great chasm spread wider and deeper, side streams cut into the plateau walls, shaping promontories. Further erosion cut in behind the peninsulas, detaching them from the main plateau in broad mesas. More cutting and weathering and mud slide and rockslide wore the mesas down to flat-topped buttes with hard limestone or sandstone caps. Some have been worn down to sharp pinnacles or have wasted away to the flat top of the next resistant layer.

Because the North Rim rises higher than the South Rim—as high as 9,000 feet—it receives more rain and snow. Because the plateau slopes southward, runoff from the north side spills down into the canyon, while south side runoff flows away from the rim. As a result, erosion has chiseled away much more of the northern wall. There rise most of the majestic buttes, hewn by nature, ordained by man as the shrines of exotic gods.

The naming bug persists. On a red rock hulk known as the Battleship, just west of Yavapai Museum, the sun at midmorning projects twin shadows that resemble human faces. A recent visitor I spoke with has named them Moses and Eve. Though they are only shadow figures, the gesture heartened me. Amid the plethora of deities and legendary colossi commemorated here, I found the Old Testament sadly underrepresented.

Others have found the whole scheme disheartening, an alien encrustation. "What a lugging in by the ears of questionable characters!" protested one critic. François Matthes, the gifted cartographer who continued the practice of "heroic nomenclature" begun by Clarence Dutton, defended it: "we compliment inanimate nature when we christen its imperfect mountain shapes for the noblest works of man's own genius."

Fortunately, in addition to the "unnaturalized foreigners," there are also many Indian names on the land, hinting at the true heritage of human presence here. Beautiful Indian wares tempt us throughout the visitor areas of the park. I studied them—and their price tags—in the curio shops: turquoise and silver jewelry and pottery from famous sites—the black-on-black from Santa Clara Pueblo, the rusty tones of Jemez ware, the lively birds and beasts and fishes adorning the Hopi Reservation pottery, the brown-on-black geometrics of the white pots from Acoma.

There are other pots, treasures beyond price locked away on park study shelves, on display in the Tusayan Museum along the East Rim Drive, scattered throughout the canyon, and at thousands of sites yet to be explored by the archaeologists—all making up the 4,000-year-old mosaic of Native American life in canyon country.

"We've recorded more than 2,600 sites, about 5 percent of what we think is here," said park archaeologist Jan Balsom when I visited her in her office. "There may be more than 50,000 in the park."

Ruins of stone pueblos, cliff shelters, cave shelters, scatters of pottery shards, and implements and weapon points of stone spread across the park's 1,904 square miles. The archaeologist's cabinets contain a trove of ollas—storage jars—and other ceramic pots, stone tools and weapon points, woven baskets and sandals, and intriguing animal figurines woven three to four thousand years ago from split twigs of squawbush, willow, and cottonwood and left by canyon dwellers in caves of Redwall limestone. Some of the figures have little spears run through them and bits of desiccated animal dung set within them. One can only guess what the ancient weavers had in mind, perhaps the desire to conjure a successful hunt.

Jan and I left the cabinets and drove eastward for some distance, then descended just below the rim to a rock overhang, a prehistoric shelter. Wary of random visitation and the risk of vandalism, Jan exacted a promise that I would not reveal the location of the site. I had no hesitation. Blessed with a miserable sense of direction, I keep such promises willy-nilly.

The shelter looked down on the canyon panorama. To the northeast, a hundred miles away, rose the shadowy bulk of Navajo Mountain. Those who dwelt here must have known many a glorious sunset. On the walls they left some 50 examples of rock art: paintings and stone peckings, pictographs and petroglyphs—human and animal figures, zigzags. Different styles, with some figures painted on top of others, indicate different periods of occupation. We speculated on what it all meant. "Everybody sees things a little differently, interprets things a little differently," said Jan. "I think one of the beauties of rock art is there's no real explanation for it.

"The Indians used the whole canyon from rim to river. Summer and early fall would be good times to be up on the rim, to get piñon nuts from the pines. In the springtime they'd want to be down in the inner canyon, to get the cactus fruits. Mesquite beans became available at different levels, generally from spring-time to early summer. They were farming up here too; we've found some terrace systems with check dams where they were channeling runoff into planted areas." Water, then as now, was a problem. The South Rim has no year-round water sources. The nearest source, other than some isolated springs in the inner canyon, said Jan, is the river—some 4,500 feet below the rim. "Nobody knows how they got their water up here."

What does the rock art signify? How did the people get water? The questions multiply. At another site Jan pointed to an isolated pinnacle of rock. Getting to it from the South Rim meant a tortuous descent and then an even rougher climb. Yet atop the pinnacle ran courses of rock slabs, obviously an array set by human hands. It is one of several high, lonely outposts in the park, with little or no evidence that they were ever used. "Nobody knows how or why they were built," observed Jan. Anthropologist Robert C. Euler, who studied them, thought they might have served as defensive fortresses, places of refuge in times of assault—somewhat like our modern bomb shelters.

Near the New Hance Trail the park planned a parking lot. Before construction began, Jan and her assistants came out to retrieve what prehistoric people had left there. I joined them there one day. The site, said Jan, contained evidence of occupation and use from the days of the Archaic peoples of 2500 B.C., to the Anasazi of around A.D. 1100, on up to historic times—the Havasupai and the Hopi in the late 1800s, the Navajo in the 1900s, even the Civilian Conservation Corps in the 1930s. The CCC had dug a borrow pit the size of a soccer field for road building, so it seemed a good place to put a parking lot. Yet amid the gravel, artifacts still turn up: a bit of chert with serrated edges for cutting, a stone drill, half-inch-long dart points that would have been used with bow and arrows, pottery shards.

Some months later Park Superintendent Jack Davis told me that the Havasupai, next-door neighbors to the park on the west, had objected to the parking lot. The site held sacred meaning for them. Out of deference, Davis said, the project was put on hold.

Near the eastern bounds of the park stand the ruins of Tusayan Pueblo, the first prehistoric site professionally documented in canyon country and the first excavated, with low stone walls tracing rooms and granaries and kiva. It dates from around 1185, said Jan, and some 30 Anasazi occupied it for 30 to 35 years, about the life expectancy of a human in those days.

The ever present plateau forest, piñon pine and juniper, grew close about.

"The forest would have been denuded when the site was occupied," Jan said. The view that prehistoric people were environmentally more sensitive to their surroundings than we are is a fallacy, according to Jan. "The Indians would have used everything available. They would have cut down the trees for building material and fire. They would have used all the plant resources, hunted all the animals they could. It's just that they couldn't do as much damage to the environment. When the resources were gone, they moved on. And the trees grew back." The departure of the people of Tusayan coincided with an overall Anasazi abandonment of the canyon. They are believed to have settled on mesas to the east, ancestors of today's Hopi people. What drove them out? Perhaps climate change that shrank already critical water supplies, or a depletion of resources through overuse, or hostile invaders. Another puzzlement.

Near the ruined pueblo and its museum, a break in a water pipe showed me what a bit of water can do on this thirsty plateau. The pool formed by the leak attracted a lively troop of birds, and I was pleased to add a spell of birding to my tour of prehistory. I picked out, more or less confidently, jays, nuthatches, towhees, and ravens. Others were simply beyond the ken of an eastern backyard birder. When I returned on another day, the avian oasis had dried up, and the birds, like the Anasazi, had vanished. Man's tinkering has added some surprising chapters to the saga of bird life in the canyon, especially deep down along the watercourses. Here on the South Rim, Stephen Whitney informs us in his *Field Guide to the Grand Canyon,* one of the best places to find birds is around the park's sewage lagoons. Ah, wilderness.

The pool formed by the leak attracted a lively troop of birds. . . . When I returned on another day, the avian oasis had dried up, and the birds, like the Anasazi, had vanished.

Of the four million annual visitors to the park, some 40,000 venture afoot into the backcountry, much of it wilderness. Eager to try it, I clattered out to the park in full regalia—state-of-the-art backpack, sleeping bag warm down to 10°F, roomy tent with floor and fly, camp stove, lantern. But the sweet heart of the watermelon out here is not the rind, at 7,000 feet above sea level, but somewhere, almost anywhere, below the rims, down steep and punishing canyon walls, down into the desert. It was not long before I heard tales of wrung-out hikers, faint of heart, wobbly of foot, dragging along in the telltale "Kaibab shuffle," gasping for breath and for water. They abandon gear and food and clothing, and sometimes they abandon the hike as well, until a patrolling ranger arrives with pep talk, water, and a trendy mix of electrolytes and other restoratives called "Gookinaid."

"People just take off into the canyon without realizing they're climbing a mountain in reverse," says ranger Bev Perry, who heads the backcountry sub-district. "The hard part comes at the end. For a long time I've wanted to build a hundred-foot ramp so that people would have to experience hiking up before they start down. If people knew what they're getting into, it would cut our medical emergencies in half."

Swiftly my strategy changed. I downsized pack and sleeping bag, retrieved a light plastic tube tent that had been waiting in the attic for a grandchild to claim it, and swallowed pride and accepted senior-citizen status whenever a companion volunteered to carry a cookstove. I never could solve the dilemma of clothing—an outing often ranged from freezing rim to scorching gorge and back again—or water, the hiker's albatross. No strategy I ever heard of could finesse the burden of three or four liters for an overnight trek, at least two of which must be saved for the up leg, always the tough one.

Whatever the advantages of senior citizenship, they pale beside those of juniors. Down on the Colorado River one day I found two-year-old Forest Nolan-Rapatz starting up the nearly one-mile-high, nine-mile-long Bright Angel Trail with nothing more than a teddy bear tucked inside his belt. "He'll go as far as he can," said his mother, Marcia Rapatz of Browerville, Minnesota, "then he'll go in here." She pointed to the kiddie pack slung just above her daypack.

On the upper course of the Hermit Trail, which heads at the western end of West Rim Drive and drops 1,400 feet in little over a mile, I was overtaken by Toft Bragg, already a veteran canyoneer at the age of eight months. He had made his first trip to the inner gorge six months before, in the (Continued on page 55)

*S*teep and treacherous, the Hopi Salt Trail through Salt Trail Canyon challenges the author and his Park Service companions. The trail leads to caves above the Colorado, where the Hopi have gathered salt for centuries.

TOM BEAN

TOM BEAN

Gnarled branches spread wide as if in welcome, a Utah juniper clings to the South Rim. Most common juniper in Arizona, it flourishes in the rocky soils of the Colorado Plateau.

Duck-on-a-Rock: The name of this limestone monolith near Yavapai Point befits its profile, the handiwork of wind and frost. A petroglyph (below) distinguishes a wall of Hopi Trail Canyon, part of a prehistoric route from the Hopi mesas west to the Colorado River. Rock carvings and paintings throughout canyon country recall the ancient Indian presence.

FOLLOWING PAGES: Thousands of feet above the Colorado, Navajo Indians tend goats and sheep on the eastern rim of Marble Canyon. The Navajo Reservation abuts Marble, the narrow northern neck of the Grand Canyon.

JERRY JACKA

46

©DAVID MUENCH 1990; DAVID HISER (FOLLOWING PAGES)

DAVID HISER (BOTH)

*N*avajo girls in traditional dress now reserved for ceremonial occasions— long skirts, velvet blouses, and handcrafted jewelry—complement the beauty of globemallow bouquets. Earrings, medallions, and belts worn by Norlena Johnson (opposite) and her sister Crystal Yazzie reflect Navajo mastery of coral, turquoise, and silver.

WILLARD CLAY

CARR CLIFTON

*R*eceding clouds of an early spring snow wreathe Isis Temple as seen from Hopi Point (left); the storm also dusted rocks far below the rim, an uncommon and short-lived event. A few miles distant, the winding Colorado River appears creek size; in reality its width at this point equals the length of a football field—300 feet. Near Grandview Point (above) piñon pines sprout from a snowy ledge worn thin by weathering and erosion.

53

same way he traveled now, on the back of his mother, Susie Bragg. She had hiked to the river often as an employee of Phantom Ranch, the only lodging in the park below the rims and a popular goal of hikers and mule riders. Toft blinked in the sunlight and smiled a greeting as his mother picked her way down the cobbled zigzags.

Turning back up Hermit Trail, I marked my progress by the layers of rock surmounted, each differing in thickness, usually in color, in texture, and, most important, in difficulty. Wearied by the steepness and the sun, I started up the Kaibab limestone with a sense of relief—the last layer, almost there. Only 600 vertical feet left to go. Only. In this canyon 600 feet represents a light jaunt; translated to an urban context, you are looking at a 60-story skyscraper—without air-conditioning.

On an April morning, a day after snow and rain had blustered over the South Rim, photographer Tom Bean and I started down the Grandview Trail (he was hauling the camp stove). This is the glory time of canyoneering, winter on the rims declining, the 100-plus temperatures down below still some weeks ahead. For popular trails, such as Grandview, in popular seasons, backcountry reservations must be made months in advance. With such lead times, of course, cancellations are not uncommon, offering some opportunities to spur-of-the-moment campers.

Three miles, 31 switchbacks, and some 2,500 vertical feet from the South Rim trailhead—a short, steep trek rated relatively easy by veterans of the canyon, though not by me—we made camp on Horseshoe Mesa. The mesa earns its name for its unmistakable shape, a huge rough horseshoe of Redwall limestone. Not far from the campsite stood the ruins of a stone shack, a vestige of the Last Chance Mine. Shafts and machinery recall the mining days elsewhere on the mesa. The copper ore ran rich, reportedly as much as 70 percent pure. In 1893 mine owner Pete Berry exhibited some of it at the Chicago World's Fair.

As we set up camp, we reveled in the mid-canyon vista, new to me, up to the rims, down the side drainages along the prongs of the horseshoe, out to the gorge of the Colorado. As the day wore on, thunder rattled across the canyon,

*S*mudged with lichens, a sandstone
rampart known as the Hopi Wall
breaks into terraces of ponderosa pine.
Seemingly invincible, the lofty crag
will eventually disappear, erased
by relentless wind, frost, and rain.

©LARRY ULRICH

and the mottled, lowering sky at times obscured the high places, the temples—cloud-capp'd towers indeed.

We headed out the western prong of the horseshoe, following kinking talus ramps down the mesa wall to the dark opening of the Cave of the Domes. Its passages run for nearly a half mile, through soaring heights of almost 50 feet, some spacious and domelike, some merely narrow shafts rising like chimneys in the rock.

*S*talagmites beside grottoes had the look of cowled figures at prayer. Weird forms jutted out from high corners: gargoyles, of course. In the gloaming, nothing is farfetched.

Bulging sidewalls, dimly detailed by our flashlights, made me think of choir lofts; stalagmites beside grottoes had the look of cowled figures at prayer. Weird forms jutted out from high corners: gargoyles, of course. In the gloaming, nothing is farfetched.

At the turn of the century, writer George Wharton James, exploring by candlelight, devised an ingenious way to photograph a stalagmite that caught his fancy. He cut up all the candles he could spare, lit 27 of the pieces, exposed the old-fashioned plate, and went off to see the rest of the cave. Several hours later he returned, covered the plate, and subsequently presented his readers "with the first and only photograph I have ever seen made by candle-light alone."

Tom Bean poked fun at my notion of a sacral ambience in the dusty cavern. But as long ago as 1898 a visitor noted the "high-arched chambers almost ecclesiastical in architecture." And the morning after our visit we crossed paths on the mesa with Dick Gaffney, of Scottsdale, Arizona, a retired engineer with a patriarchal white beard, enjoying another of his periodic canyon treks. A year earlier Dick had led a party of 18, including his fiancée and a minister, down Grandview, picked out a big, domed room in the Cave of the Domes, got married—and had a fine wedding party right there. And hiked out the same day, the backcountry procession and recession totaling six miles.

Though many caves pierce the Redwall and some other rock layers, the Cave of the Domes is one of the few open to visitors without a special permit.

Some people I talked with called it a "sacrifice" cave, heavily vandalized in the past and now open without restriction. Some of its stalagmites and stalactites went to adorn the front porch of the Grandview Hotel, which Pete Berry built at the trailhead in 1895.

Peter Rowlands, then chief of resource management, told me the park is reluctant even to reveal the locations of caves, to protect not merely their beauty but also their archaeological and paleontological riches—treasures such as the split-twig figurines found on Horseshoe Mesa and elsewhere, or the 11,000-year-old fossil bones of giant condors discovered in remote caverns of the Redwall.

Another day, another descent, another tale of a precious park resource at risk: the very air that courses through and over the Grand Canyon. Unpolluted, it is one of the most pristine pockets in the lower 48, especially in winter; visual range may extend 200 miles or more, limited only by the curvature of the earth.

But the canyon air is often polluted, which is how I came to be starting down the South Kaibab Trail with a group that included Dave Dietrich, the president of a consulting firm in Fort Collins, Colorado. The South Kaibab Trail, like the Bright Angel Trail, serves as a major corridor for hikers and mule riders between the South Rim and Phantom Ranch. No one was surprised when Dave Dietrich quickly fell behind. He labored under a bulging load of cameras and associated gear—80 pounds of metal—and he was pitching sweat within minutes of the trailhead. Set on a canyon butte and automated, the cameras would gather yet more data in the years-long campaign to document the air quality of the Grand Canyon, especially the effect of sulfur dioxides spewed from the 77-story stacks of the Navajo Generating Station.

Ironically, the coal-burning plant at Page, Arizona, just beyond the northeastern end of the canyon, had been built as the consequence of an environmental triumph. In a campaign that rang across the nation, environmentalists had beat back a plan to build two power dams within the Grand Canyon—one at Marble Canyon, the other at Bridge Canyon. Instead, the plant at Page would generate electricity, consuming as much as 24,000 tons of coal a day. Its sulfur emissions are not the only source of pollutants. Summer winds waft in haze from urban agglomerations in southern California. But the Park Service has concluded, after years of study, that the Page plant is a "significant contributor" to winter haze, reducing visibility and obscuring details of the magnificent vistas. Nearly a million people visit the canyon in wintertime.

The Environmental Protection Agency has endorsed the findings and, invoking the Clean Air Act, has proposed a ruling ordering the plant to greatly reduce sulfur dioxide emissions. Faced with emission control costs that may run as high as two billion dollars, the plant owners—a consortium of public and private utilities and the Bureau of Reclamation, a sister agency of the Park Service—vigorously challenge the validity of the scientific data and the EPA ruling.

Yet, Park Superintendent Jack Davis told me, "There's really been no credible challenge to the Park Service studies to date. I feel very strongly that we can't have a single source like that doing what it's doing to one of the most spectacular scenes in the world. We need to take every step possible to correct it."

The power lines stream out from Page, slung on gigantic towers, spreading across the enormous Navajo Indian Reservation, ignoring lonely hogans without power. Not far from Page the Glen Canyon Dam impounds Colorado River water for distant cities and fields. On the Marble Platform, at the eastern edge of canyon country, I rode rutted roads past hogans without water. Jimmy Young grew up here; his kinfolk still live in the hogans. To get water, they drive to The Gap, 30 miles away. Yet even on this sere, sagy plateau east of Marble Canyon, may the people, as the Navajo say, "Walk in Beauty."

I camped here one night, awoke to find my plastic tube stiff with frost, piled dead sagebrush on a fire to fight the chill, sipped coffee, and watched the sun come up out of the Painted Desert under a gaudy sky, a grand effusion of turquoise. Teddy Roosevelt passed through this country and recorded some Navajo prayers, one of which fit this moment: "Dawn, beautiful dawn, the Chief, This day, let it be well with me as I go."

"Take me back. That's where I was born and that's where I like to be." And that's where he passed away, on the brushy limestone bench, under the turquoise.

Jimmy's grandfather grew old in a hogan here. "I took him to my home in Page," Jimmy told me. "A fine home. I sat him in front of a television. Fed him good. He stayed about two weeks. You could see he wasn't eating. I said, 'What's wrong?' He said, 'Take me back. That's where I was born and that's where I like to be.' " And that's where he passed away, on the brushy limestone bench, under the turquoise.

To hike the rough trails down the Marble Canyon wall to the Colorado requires permits from the park and from the Navajo nation. The boundary is disputed; both claim the canyon wall. Southward the Salt Trail Canyon lies entirely within the Navajo reservation, leading down to the Little Colorado River. Whenever runoff has not muddied its waters, this stretch of the *Colorado Chiquito* conveys the azure outpourings of Blue Spring, rich in calcium carbonate, through a steep, sinuous canyon to the bigger Colorado and the Grand Canyon.

There are several ways to see the surprising Little Colorado. River runners coming down from Lees Ferry on the Colorado often pause at the confluence. Then there's a test track for rodeo broncs, which some call a road, leading from the easternmost park overlook at Desert View to Cape Solitude. One day a party of us in a four-wheel drive zipped over the 20 miles in 2 hours. Those are the easy ways. There's also the route through Salt Trail Canyon. It is a small segment of a 100-mile trail followed by Hopis for centuries, a ritual pilgrimage from their mesas in the east to the salt deposits in the Grand Canyon. I have heard from Hopis that the journey is still made. These traditional people prefer not to discuss details, for the journey includes a stop at their sacred shrine of emergence, the *sipapu,* a low travertine cone containing a bubbling yellow pool. Here, according to tradition, the first Hopis emerged from the lower world.

In a published account of a pilgrimage in 1912, one young Hopi remembered his first descent into Salt Trail Canyon: It "seemed miles deep. . . . I was frightened and wondered if we would ever return in safety. The War Chief said, 'Line up for prayers.'"

Prayers never hurt. It also helps to line up plenty of water, route descriptions, and, above all, companions like Bev Perry and her assistant, park ranger Ken Phillips, a hard-core canyon hiker. By arrangement with the tribe, park rangers familiarize themselves with areas adjacent to the boundary where they may be summoned on emergency calls.

Let no evil cross our path, the Hopi pilgrims prayed. We spent nearly ten hours in Salt Trail Canyon one day. No evil crossed; it lay right on the path, often only a faint path, often marked by stone cairns. Steep talus switchbacks and narrow, exposed ledges made for some of the meanest scrambling I encountered in all of my canyon journeys. "Stumble here," said Bev, "and you can kiss yourself goodbye."

I looked for the landmarks of the Hopi narratives. Broad, slanting slabs of Coconino sandstone that required wide strides seemed to match the place called Spreading Buttocks, an evil bit of ledge with a bulging overhang that required some rock hugging and a gingerly step across—the "Nose-scraping Place," no doubt. We left our packs at a campsite on a lofty bench and jinked down another talus slope to complete the 5-mile, 2,700-foot descent to the Little Colorado. It ran true blue, over creamy little islets, gurgling down dams of travertine, a touch of the tropics, a mirage, no desert at all. But new evils stalked the riverside path—muddy banks, rockfalls, cat-claw acacia that left its signature in bright pink scrawls on arms and legs, blockades of the exotic tamarisk exactly as guidebook author John Annerino described them: "dense stands of tammies where the popular breaststroke is required to make any headway."

Don't drink the water, my companions had warned; it's limy and probably contaminated. Then my flask ran dry, with perhaps an hour or more and a rugged ascent before we reached the reserves at camp. Drink the water, they said.

What about *Giardia?* I asked. It takes a couple of weeks for the symptomatic queasiness to appear, they replied. Worry about the bacteria later; when you hike here, you've got to have water.

I filled my flask with the milky blue water and gulped it down. The Little Colorado looks a lot better than it tastes, but it did the job. And whatever was in it did no harm. I never did get queasy.

*J*ust west of the park, in a tight side canyon coursed by another beautiful blue stream, dwell the Havasupai— the "People of the Blue-green Water."

Two other Indian reservations hem the Grand Canyon's South Rim. Just west of the park, in a tight side canyon coursed by another beautiful blue stream, dwell the Havasupai—the "People of the Blue-green Water." Havasu Creek spills down a series of enchanting waterfalls and, like the Little Colorado, blends its blue waters with the main stream of the Grand Canyon. For some seven centuries the Havasupai have centered their life here amid their sacred rock towers, farming, gathering wild plants, hunting, running stock on the adjacent plateaus. Today they welcome guests to a campground and modern lodge. Visitors come by helicopter, on horseback, or on foot in a ten-mile hike to the campground. The canyon of the Havasupai remains roadless.

For nearly a century the Havasupai Reservation had been squeezed into a section of Havasu Canyon, a wedge of 518 acres. The tribe struggled for years to enlarge it. Then in 1975, when the national park was extended to nearly twice its size to include Grand Canyon and Marble Canyon National Monuments, the Havasupai won an expansion of 185,000 acres. The increase seems enormous, 350 times bigger than the canyon wedge, but there may be less there than meets the eye. By law the land must be kept forever wild, restricted mainly to traditional use, essentially grazing. In effect the Havasupai, numbering more than 600 members, today own the plateau grazing lands they had been using all along with permits from the former owner, the national park.

To the west of the Havasupai for 108 miles, the walls and the South Rim of the Grand Canyon lie within the domain of the Hualapai Indians. Half the width of the Colorado River too, say the Hualapai. No part of the river, says the park. Here also, as in Navajo country, the boundary remains in dispute. The Hualapai indisputably own a ragged crescent of a million acres, plateau and canyon land, and there's a lot going on out there.

Hualapai boatmen run river trips. Other river runners ramp on and ramp off at Diamond Creek by permission of the Hualapai, who own the only road that runs down to the Colorado in the entire 277-mile stretch of the Grand Canyon. With a three-dollar permit anyone can drive the 23 miles to the canyon bottom. Helicopters rendezvous with river runners by permission of the Hualapai, who own the only nongovernment rights to land in the canyon.

Hualapai guides lead trophy hunters who pay almost $20,000 each for a chance to down a bighorn ram—with no guarantees.

Timber managers estimate the reservation has about 50,000 acres of harvestable ponderosa pine and another 40,000 acres of piñon and juniper that look promising for the West Coast fuelwood market.

At the northwestern corner of the reservation, on the canyon rim, stands a huge tower of girders and cross struts and loose sheet metal clanking in the wind. A generation ago it powered a 9,820-foot cable tram that hauled bat guano, a rich source of fertilizer, from a cave across the Colorado. Today, against the back wall of the tower rests the dining room of Grand Canyon West, a Hualapai tourist operation. Each day visitors from Las Vegas land at a nearby strip. Hualapai in colorful shirts and dresses, traditional tribal garb, greet the visitors, give them a tour of canyon views, tell of the Hualapai way of life, and feed them barbecued beef and fixings.

Tribal Vice Chairman Edgar Walema told me of an ambitious project on the eastern side of the reservation, also on the rim, not far from Lava Falls, the climactic rapid on the river. Here the tribe proposes to build a combination observatory-resort. "It will have a capacity for perhaps 3,000 guests," Walema said, "and every guest room will have a telescope of its own." There would also be a huge observatory telescope, and each guest could see what it sees on television screens.

Does the park object to any of this? I asked. "The Park Service questions a lot of things we do," Walema replied, "but all of this, from midstream of the Colorado River, this land is ours, and the Park Service doesn't have any say."

Some 400 breccia pipes have been identified on the reservation, and exploration for uranium has begun. Is there any problem with sacred lands? I wondered. "What is considered sacred?" countered Walema. "And how does that sacredness contribute to the tribe's economy? Right now we have about 70 percent unemployment on the reservation." He admitted, however, that some of the nearly 1,500 Hualapai take sharp exception to development plans.

"I just hate to see such a good and beautiful piece of country ruined by mining," said Clay Bravo, a Hualapai cowboy and hunting guide. I had watched him and his brother Mario on horseback, and a helicopter and some helpers on foot, spend an arduous day rounding up wild horses that had been competing with bighorn sheep for food and water in Mohawk Canyon. Now we stood in shade, letting the sweat dry, and Clay glanced around at the soaring ridges. "You know," he said, "I don't think our tribe is that poor. If we just opened our eyes, we're really rather rich in what we have. There's not always a monetary value to things."

"At the violet hour . . . when the human engine waits like a taxi throbbing." Many an evening on the South Rim brought poet T. S. Eliot's image to mind. Often the violet hour coincided with the dinner hour, creating a tension of sorts. In the park, tables in the elegant dining room of the historic El Tovar Hotel are filled, except for some silly hour such as nine. I sought out the cafeterias, where the human engine may be fueled much more quickly and cheaply. Then one day I tried a different tack—accepted the silly hour and enjoyed the violet hour on the rim walk, a glorious promenade that links some of the overlooks.

Violet and gold and rose and forest green and scowling, apoplectic red splayed across the buttes and pinnacles and terraces as sunlight drained from the canyon. At a lonely spot near Grandeur Point a couple of young Australians in their 20s approached. "Is there a riling where you can get close to the edge and look out over?" asked Stephen.

Not far off, I said, but the edge here doesn't have much of a drop. Chris, the bolder of the two, made for it, then summoned Stephen so that I could take their picture.

When Stephen neared the edge, Chris grabbed him playfully. "Don't muck around!" Stephen shouted, pulling away. And when he heard the shutter click, he dashed up to the walk. "Kept me fingers crossed," he whispered.

The canyon became a sea of silhouetted crags under a golden mist. The dinner hour was long gone—and well spent. Time now for the silly hour—and dinner.

Time now, also, for a walk that would take days instead of hours and span close to two billion years of earth history. Time to explore—I end as I began, with Shakespeare's Prospero—"the dark backward and the abysm of time."

*R*avens take a respite from soaring. The scavengers haunt every corner of the canyon, from the river to the highest elevations. They frequently engage in aerial acrobatics on the thermal updrafts near the rim.

©JOHN TELFORD 1990

GEORGE H. H. HUEY

TOM BEAN

*S*unset glow of Yaki Point and the
far horizon overpower subtler hues
of twilight. Few visitors soon forget
the canyon's moods of spectacular
color, ever changing patterns of light
and shadow moving from dawn to
dusk across angular battlements and
rounded spires. Jeffrey Hughes
crawls out on remote Pinal Point to
photograph a fleeting blaze of beauty.

TOM BEAN

Moonrise illumines subtle stripes of sandstone and shale on Vishnu Temple.
The 7,635-foot butte, crowned with limestone, once formed part of the North Rim.

MICHAEL COLLIER

©JERRY SIEVE

*C*omanche Point (opposite)
commands 140 miles of canyon.
Kaibab limestone formed 250 million
years ago caps the formation. From
Hopi Point, older Redwall limestone
(above) zigzags in a bold blush
between the rim and the river.

Mule riders descend into the canyon on the Bright Angel Trail, an ancient Havasupai footpath and famous South Rim route. The popularity of mule trips requires booking months ahead. Four million tourists visit Grand Canyon National Park each year. Rangers, like Tom Forster, help them put the awesome setting in perspective.

FOLLOWING PAGES: At rainbow's end, Sumner Butte overlooks two hikers on the 7-mile-long South Kaibab Trail.

TOM BEAN (BOTH); RALPH LEE HOPKINS (FOLLOWING PAGES)

Rim to Rim

*O*oh Aah Point, on the South Rim, lives up to its name
at sunset. Trails connect disparate worlds—the scrub
dryness of the South Rim and the forest-shaded North Rim.

GEORGE LAMONT; DAVID HISER (PRECEDING PAGES)

Winter morning's glow warms Cheops Pyramid; the broad terrace of the Tonto Platform flares at its flanks. Beyond, at left, Isis Temple broods in shadow.

How far to the North Rim, the hard-edged line that bounds the far side of the canyon? Line of sight is shortest, ten miles from the sightseers' promenade on the South Rim. Driving is longest, a roundabout of 215 miles. Trail miles are hardest and best: down through the abyss of time, rim to river to rim, evergreen to cactus to lush streamside and on up to conifers again—an array of plant life representative of Mexican desert and Canadian forest in a stretch of 20-odd miles. Park trails present a variety of options, from turnpike arteries with footbridges spanning the Colorado and the creeks to wilderness footpaths where hikers hitch ferry rides on river runners' boats; unwisely, some float across on one- or two-man rafts.

My friend Scott Thybony, who knows the river and the rocks and the routes and writes about them, suggested one of the wild routes, the South Bass Trail. It was constructed at the turn of the century by William Wallace Bass, who mined asbestos and led pack trips across the Colorado on a cable ferry to his camp, garden, and fruit orchard, and on up to the North Rim. The ferry is long gone; today, finding the trail is an adventure. It requires a two-hour drive west of the park village, on uncertain roads, impassable when wet, through Kaibab National Forest and Havasupai tribal lands. The last leg is so rough that the hike may begin three miles from the trailhead.

Few visitors venture out to—or even know about—such lonely reaches of the park. Just east of the Bass trailhead juts Havasupai Point, another scenic exclamation point on the rim, superb for camping. Here lies the Grand Scenic Divide, which sets off the chop of mesas and buttes and the greenish Tonto Platform to the east from the terraces dominated by the broad red bench of the Esplanade running westward. There's an interesting mélange of names around here too—King Arthur Castle and Holy Grail Temple, where William Bass's ashes were strewn, and Darwin Plateau, Evolution Amphitheater, and Fossil Mountain.

Scott and I day-hiked a bit in this vicinity, dropping down rubbly slopes from Point Huitzil, picking our way around scraggly piñon, links of prickly pear, and daggers of yucca. We crawled into a crevice of rock and down a length of log, its limbs trimmed to form a stepladder, possibly set there by Indians to

Descending toward the depths of the canyon, hikers on the South Kaibab Trail navigate steep switchbacks. A journey from rim to rim usually takes two days and cuts through a kaleidoscope of rock formations.

DAVID HISER

provide access to nearby granaries and shelter overhangs. In them we found a fire ring next to a pile of deer antlers, perhaps a hunting shrine. We stood on a sloping ledge where in times past artists had stood, laboriously pecking figures and designs into the sandstone ledge and adjacent cliff wall—petroglyphs of birds, of human figures, some upside down, some that seemed to be leaping with arms outstretched. The trail back to the rim was tiresome though fairly clear, but once we got there, it took a few compass readings and some shinnying up trees to rendezvous with the van.

For a cross-canyon hike the constraints of the desert and the northern forest, to say nothing of weak knees, steered me away from such far-out routes. The desert of the inner canyon does not welcome summer backpackers. Early fall is an ideal time to visit. North Rim climate rules out most of the rest of the year; the park there closes in late October, reopens around mid-May, winter permitting. I have heard, but do not choose to believe, that there are those who backpack skis (and food and shelter and cookware) across the canyon and ski the 45 miles between the northern trailhead and the highway at Jacob Lake. In May, around the time the North Rim opens, rangers start shaking their heads about the heat of the inner gorge.

So it came to pass, one day near the middle of May, that geologist William Breed, photographer David Hiser, and I, slightly a-shiver from the cold, shouldered packs down the South Kaibab Trail. We had chosen a well-trodden route, applied months earlier for a site at a well-appointed campground, and reserved meals at Phantom Ranch to cut the weight of our burden.

The South Kaibab drops more than 4,700 feet in some 7 miles. More than most trails, it shuns defiles, descending along open promontories and ridges, and offering a feast of canyon vistas—but no water and scarcely any shade. It was built to foil the power of Ralph Cameron, a U.S. senator from Arizona whose old mining claims enabled him to levy a toll of a dollar a head on users of the Bright Angel Trail, today the busiest route of all, and costing nothing but sweat.

Starting below the hotel cluster, the Bright Angel takes a bit over 9 miles to drop 4,460 feet, often between sheer canyon walls. It offers more shade and a gentler pitch, with a campground midway and water supplies along the trail during the busy season. For round-trippers, conventional wisdom dictates, "Down the South Kaibab, up the Bright Angel." We were heading straight across, with a stop at Bright Angel Campground near Phantom Ranch, then up the North Kaibab Trail, the canyon artery to the opposite rim.

Bill Breed studied earth history in this matchless sweep of "layer-cake geology." In his more than two decades as head of the geology department at the Museum of Northern Arizona, Bill has added much to the store of knowledge of canyon country. Over the years he has occasionally tried to pass some of it on to me. Bill is a patient man. Early on, he set the tone and pace of our hike. "Most people coming down here," he said, "are just interested in getting from top to bottom. There are so many things to see; if you go too fast, you miss a lot. I've never been one to set records." I found the distractions more than aesthetic or educational; they are also psychotherapeutic, taking your mind off the knee-hammering descent.

We started down the gray cliff of Kaibab limestone, away from the cutting edge of the morning wind that raked the canyon rim. "In a sense the Kaibab formation is the most important one in the canyon," Bill said. "If it wasn't for the Kaibab, the canyon wouldn't look like it does. In arid climates like this, limestone is very resistant to erosion, so it forms a caprock, not only for the canyon but also for much of northern Arizona."

The two rock formations just below the Kaibab—the Toroweap, similar to it, and the very different Coconino sandstone—are also resistant. "If those three weren't here," said Bill, "the canyon would be much wider, wouldn't be as dramatic." Above the limestone caprock some 2,000 feet of rock formations representing about 100 million years of earth history have eroded away. The erosion started some 70 million years ago, when earth forces began to push up the Colorado Plateau. Before the uplift the Kaibab limestone lay below sea level. Today it stands more than a mile above.

The rock layer just on top of the Kaibab limestone, noted Bill, "was a shale and sandstone formation—easily eroded. As someone said, as easy as a firehose scrubbing mud off concrete." That shale layer marked the beginning of the Mesozoic era, the time when dinosaurs ruled the earth. So the rimrock of the canyon, the youngest layer, is older than the dinosaurs; but relics of giant reptiles are not far away, in the stairstep of plateaus rising to the north in Utah, and just to the east, on Navajo land in the Painted Desert.

That shale layer marked the beginning of the Mesozoic era . . . when dinosaurs ruled the earth. So the rimrock of the canyon, the youngest layer, is older than the dinosaurs.

Scott Thybony and I bounced out to the Painted Desert to find them one day. In a rented four-wheel drive, fortified by jazz tapes and cold drinks, we meandered by hoodooed cliffs, slot canyons in slickrock, chunks of petrified wood, soaring crescents of barchan sand dunes, to desert cliffs "painted" white and pink and gray and brown. There, on a red-brown patch of rock, we pored over scores of three-toed footprints, some measuring more than a dozen inches from the heel to the tip of the longest toe. *Tsídii nabitiin*—bird tracks, the Navajo called them. Studies indicate, however, that the tracks were left in a mud flat more than 180 million years ago by *Dilophosaurus*, a carnivorous dinosaur somewhat like the better known *Tyrannosaurus*, but with a double-crested head.

W*e trod the hardened dregs of ancient seas; at that time . . . the floating plates of earth's crust had come together to form the supercontinent of Pangaea. . . .*

Fossils of the Grand Canyon are far different. Through the upper levels we trod the hardened dregs of ancient seas; at that time the region lay near the Equator, when the floating plates of earth's crust had come together to form the supercontinent of Pangaea, long before the continents as we know them began to take shape. The Kaibab and Toroweap rocks are rich in marine fossils representing more than 80 genera of sea creatures—corals, brachiopods (primitive bivalves like clams), sponges, snails, fish. Much of this marine life we know only from fossils, for the canyon rim marks a great divide in earth history—the end of the Permian period and of the Paleozoic era, when a vast and puzzling extinction of more than half the existing families of marine invertebrates occurred.

Bill traced the fossils of a sponge and a brachiopod embedded in the rock, and, as we hiked the hairpins, took note of the living things that grew alongside the trail: gooseberry and skunkbush, cliff rose and Mormon tea, paintbrush in bloom, a mat of locoweed. "It's in the pea family," he said of the latter. "Horses eat it and go crazy. It causes permanent brain damage. Locoed horses are totally unpredictable; they've been known to run into trees or over cliffs."

The morning chill and a haze hung in the air as we entered the steepening switchbacks that hug the white cliff of Coconino sandstone. The Coconino is a standout layer. When a low sun kindles the upper canyon walls, the Coconino seems to burn brightest—a band of light—often reminding me of the high, bright clerestory of a cathedral. The Coconino cliff also stands out as one of the toughest stretches on the trail. And, unlike most of the other rock, the Coconino formed from desert dunes, windblown sands that were carried upslope, then dropped on the lee side of the dunes to form cross beds, easily seen in the rock today. The Coconino spreads across most of northern Arizona, and this great desert may have been near the west coast of Pangaea.

Fossil skeletons have not shown up in the Coconino, but there was life in that prehistoric duneland. At one point Bill stopped to search the trailside sandstone. "I'm looking for reptile tracks," he said. He had seen them at this spot many times, and now they were gone. "Vandals. I heard they chipped them off and took them away. A shame."

Scorpions and reptiles left their spoor in the ancient desert in the form of trails and tracks. Most of the reptiles were heading up the dunes. "There was a great controversy at one time about why those little critters were all heading uphill," Bill recalled. "Some said they were all males, heading for females, or maybe there was a water supply in that direction.

"Eddie McKee, being a little more of a scientist, built a sand dune in the lab and let some chuckwallas wander around on it. He found out that when they go uphill, they go slowly and laboriously. When they go downhill, they slide down like little boys and destroy their own tracks." You hear a lot about Eddie McKee at the canyon. You read a lot about him. You read a lot by Dr. Edwin D. McKee, legendary hiker, park naturalist, and scientist whose tracks are all over the research tomes of canyon geology. He died in 1984 and lies buried in the cemetery beside the South Rim Visitor Center.

Below the Coconino sandstone the South Kaibab Trail flattened out as we hiked down through the softer, slope-forming Hermit shale, red rock that once was a semiarid delta land, often flooded, roamed by reptiles and amphibians. It was a land where ferns and conifers grew, where dragonflies whirred on wings that spanned nearly a foot. On the shaley flat of Cedar Ridge a hummingbird whistled by; we could not see its colors, but the metallic trilling gave it away—the sound of the beating wings of a male broad-tailed hummingbird.

Under the Hermit shale lie more red beds, a lot more, though not as easy to differentiate. The Supai group runs about 900 vertical feet, terraced steps now plunging, now sloping, through layers hard and soft—sandstone, shale, limestone—the slopes strewn with talus eroded from above. There is evidence of ancient rivers, lagoons, and shallow seas in the Supai.

Iron oxides put the red in the red beds, giving the canyon much of its enchanting glow. The iron ores also gave data for revolutionary ideas in geology. In the 1950s scientists studied the changing magnetic orientation of the ancient minerals and compared it to present-day magnetic north. The iron oxides point to a different north polar region from the one that exists today. The data, said Bill Breed, as we twisted down the Supai terraces, "could only be explained by wandering continents. This helped to clarify the ideas of continental drift, which developed into the theory of plate tectonics. It was the start of the work that unified geology the way evolution unified biology." *(Continued on page 90)*

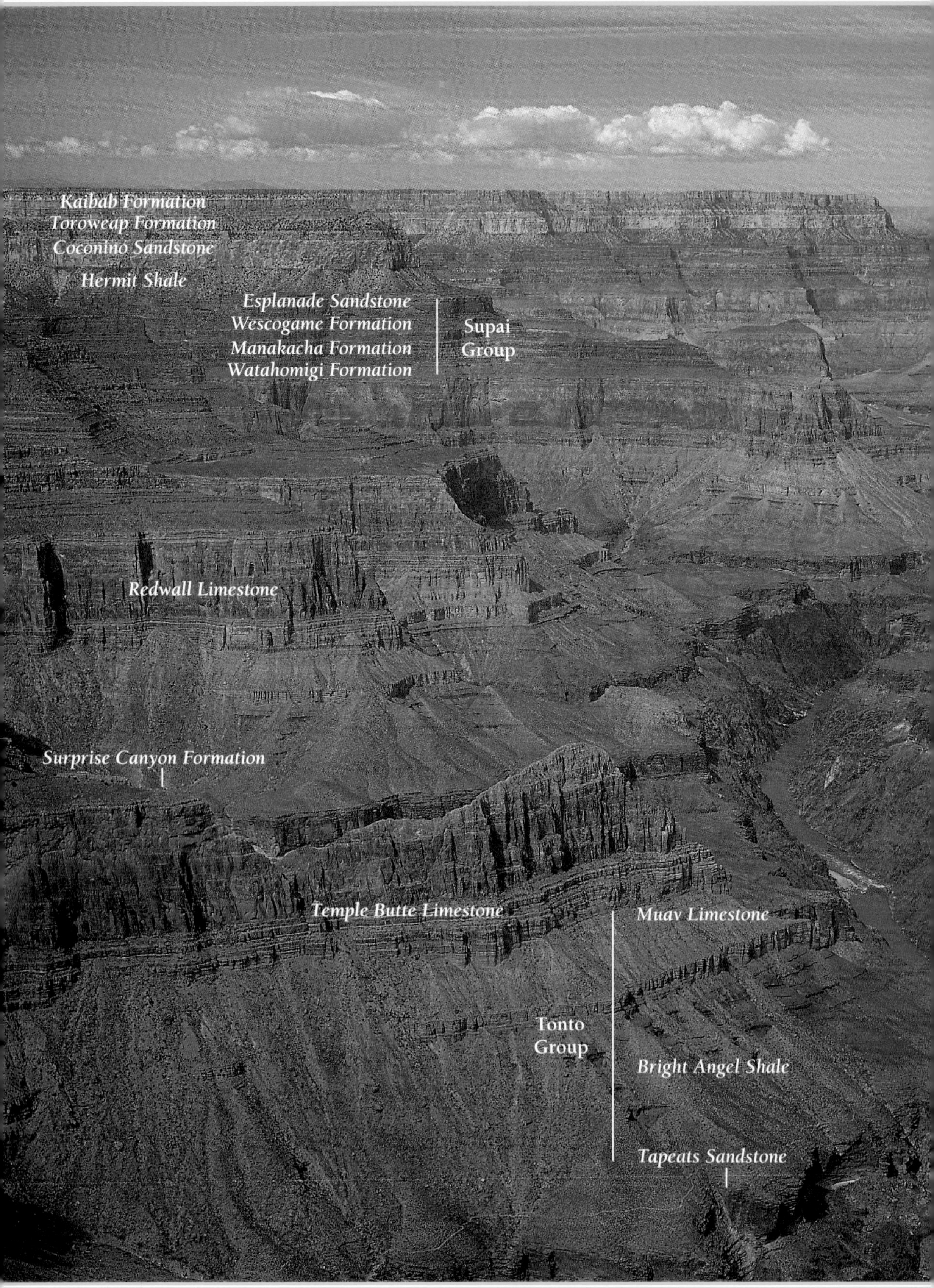

Kaibab Formation
Toroweap Formation
Coconino Sandstone

Hermit Shale

Esplanade Sandstone
Wescogame Formation
Manakacha Formation
Watahomigi Formation

Supai
Group

Redwall Limestone

Surprise Canyon Formation

Temple Butte Limestone

Muav Limestone

Tonto
Group

Bright Angel Shale

Tapeats Sandstone

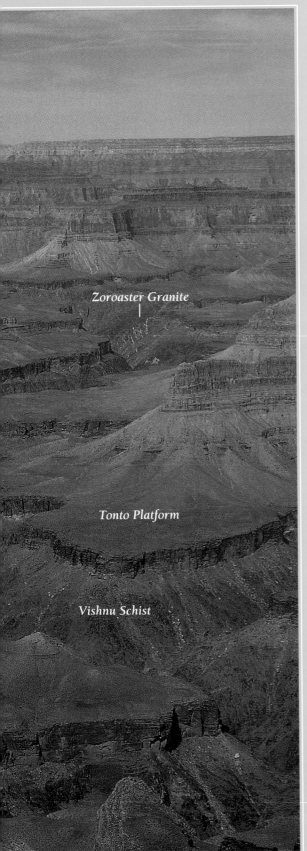

Zoroaster Granite

Tonto Platform

Vishnu Schist

MICHAEL COLLIER (BOTH)

Geology

A Portfolio

A "dark and mysterious cleaving," an early river runner called the Grand Canyon. Here the cutting edge, the Colorado River, foams over Hermit Rapids in a downstream view from Mohave Point on the South Rim in Grand Canyon National Park.

Running water, heat and frost, gravity, abrasion, uplift, and faulting all combined to create the great chasm as well as its dizzying cross-hatching of side canyons.

Dark the cleaving, mysterious its subtly changing moods—yet to geologists the canyon has presented a landscape of enlightenment from John Wesley Powell's day to this.

Its "layer-cake geology" reveals more than 1.2 billion years of stratified rock in chronological sequence— younger above, older below. In the upper layers lies evidence of rich marine life; in the deepest rock layer, Vishnu schist (above) yields no record of life—though it may flaunt the artistry of the river and abrasive rocks.

Marine deposits laid down over 45 million years in a broad, clear sea

85

TOM TILL; BELOW, LEFT TO RIGHT: PAT O'HARA / DRK PHOTO; MICHAEL COLLIER; MICHAEL COLLIER; TOM TILL; ©PAT O'HARA; MICHAEL COLLIER

CANYON ROCK PORTRAITS:

WATAHOMIGI FORMATION (SUPAI GROUP)

BRACHIOPODS IN REDWALL LIMESTONE

RIVER-POLISHED VISHNU SCHIST

formed resistant Redwall limestone (the sheer cliff at left); Muav limestone (in front of the Redwall), formed in shallower seas, erodes in a gentler pattern of cliffs and slopes and ledges.

In Powell's day, scientists believed the Colorado was born, took its present course, and began canyon cutting at least 50 million years ago. Today, geologists envision a much younger canyon, though precise evidence is hard to find.

Many circumstantial clues, writes Ivo Lucchitta of the U.S. Geological Survey, enable us "to construct a solid history that has a good chance of being correct, at least in its major aspects." Lucchitta estimates the cutting of the canyon took 1.7 to 4.5 million years. To carve the Grand Canyon in less than two million years would mean the removal of 3.2 million cubic yards of rock per year, cutting downward at the "truly remarkable" rate of 3.2 feet every thousand years. ■

ESPLANADE SANDSTONE (SUPAI GROUP)

DOX SANDSTONE (GRAND CANYON SUPERGROUP)

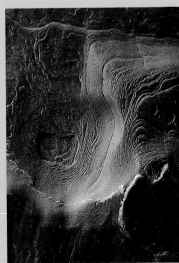

FOLIATED VISHNU SCHIST

A CLIMBER SCRAMBLES ACROSS A WALL OF VISHNU SCHIST AND PINK GRANITE.

TOM BEAN

We hit a gentle stretch of the Supai, the sunglow cooled by a freshening breeze, the air perfumed by the baby-powder fragrance of creamy blooms of cliff rose—all had the feeling of a morning constitutional on a perfect spring day. Even the mule strings, laden with packs or tourists, for which we had to step aside, could not disturb it. Ferde Grofé, I thought, had caught the horsey rhythms well in the "On the Trail" movement of his *Grand Canyon Suite:* Dum de Dum de Dum de-de-de-de Dum accenting a blithe melody. That's the way it went for bipeds too, on this down-canyon cakewalk.

"We're near the bottom of the Supai," said Bill. "This is where the Surprise Canyon formation occurs." It was nowhere in sight, for the newest discovery among the canyon's rock layers appears only in isolated rock channels. It may be seen near Three-Mile Rest House on the Bright Angel Trail and in thicker deposits in the western part of the canyon—where geologist George Billingsley spotted its distinctive red-brown outcrops in 1976.

The discovery site had already been named, and aptly so, Surprise Canyon. The 320-million-year-old rock, which seems to have formed in a web of estuarial river valleys, preserved an abundance and variety of fossils, from leaves and tree trunks to microscopic organisms and clams, snails, corals, sea lilies, mosslike bryozoans, even sharks' teeth. Some were species previously unknown in the canyon.

The trail steepened in the switchbacks of the Redwall limestone, the relentless cliff so harsh to hikers upward bound. Heading down, we could concentrate instead on the richness of its hues. . . .

The trail steepened in the switchbacks of the Redwall limestone, the relentless cliff so harsh to hikers upward bound. Heading down, we could concentrate instead on the richness of its hues, on its dominant swath in the architecture of the great chasm. "The Redwall is the most massive limestone layer in the canyon," remarked Bill, "so obviously this was the time when the seas that came over the land lasted the longest."

Beyond the Redwall we headed down through the layers deposited by Cambrian seas from 505 to 570 million years ago—the Muav limestone, the Bright Angel shale that eroded back to form the greenish flat known as the Tonto

Platform, and the dark brown Tapeats sandstone. In places the distinctive Tapeats cliff crops up against tilted younger Precambrian layers known as the Grand Canyon supergroup. Elsewhere these layers have eroded away, and the Tapeats sits directly on the dark V of the inner gorge—the jumbled older Precambrian bedrock of black Vishnu schist and red Zoroaster granite. There a hand may reach from 570-million-year-old sandstone to 1.7-billion-year-old schist, a gap in the geologic record of nearly 1.2 billion years. It is known as the Great Unconformity.

In full glare the Tonto Platform is a withering place, an almost treeless desert with touches of the Mojave and the Great Basin, home to cactus, yucca, agave, mesquite, and broad patches of blackbrush. Despite its flatness, people tend to take a breather here. Marty Weis seemed disinclined to slow up, though he was heading uphill, until I hailed him.

"Does it surprise you when people stop you?" I asked.

"It happens," he replied. "I guess you could say I'm sort of different to be seen down here." He was a strapping 28-year-old, between jobs, who lived on the South Rim. One leg was gone; he leaned on crutches. How long had he been this way? we wondered. "November 30, 1979," he said, without pause and without emotion. "Drunk driver. Driving at night with his lights out. Tried to pass me." And then: "I'm a hiker, always been a hiker. Before, and after." He turned uphill, 3,000 feet to climb.

Love of hiking will do it. So will other kinds of love. A youth in the Permian enamored of a maid in the Precambrian may fly on Cupid's wings through geologic time. I first encountered this phenomenon while toiling through the agony of Jacob's Ladder on the Bright Angel Trail. A young hiker broke his swifter pace to chat. "If you told me a year ago that I'd be hustling up and down this trail," he laughed, "I'd have said you're crazy." He had met a girl from Phantom Ranch—and soon became a frequent flier.

Of all the powerful attractants that lured Eddie McKee into the canyon, not the least was Barbara Hastings. "It was the summer of 1929," she recalled, when I phoned her one day at her home in Littleton, Colorado. "I was helping collect small mammals on the North Rim; he was the park naturalist on the South Rim. On one of his days off he just walked down the south side and up the north. It was the fastest anybody had ever done it up to then." He took about eight hours, she thought. What was the rush? "We had just gotten engaged," she said slowly. She remembered the betrothal too. Both had come down to Phantom Ranch. "We sat beside the creek with our feet in the water. And he proposed. He said he chose the canyon because there I couldn't get away. And I quickly accepted because I was afraid he might not ask again." I held the receiver a moment listening to silence. "Oh!" Barbara McKee suddenly exclaimed. "You have brought back some of the most wonderful memories of my life."

Ranger Bryan Wisher continues the tradition of the fleet-footed swains. In the summer of 1990, with work days at Phantom Ranch alternating between a pre-dawn and a mid-morning start, Bryan hiked out every other afternoon to visit Kim Besom on the South Rim. Two hours up; down the next morning in time to start work at ten. Once he hiked out in an hour and 45 minutes with a 55-pound pack, a record for the South Kaibab as far as anyone knows.

At midday Bill Breed, David Hiser, and I scoured the trail not for fossils and flowers but for a sliver of shade. Finding it in a curve of canyon wall, we sat down to eat and drink. Then on to Panorama Point amid the brightest red rock of all—Hakatai shale, one of those tilted layers in the Grand Canyon supergroup. Our goal lay just below—the Colorado, green and feisty, splaying off a boulder beach. Joining the river was Bright Angel Creek, fringed with cottonwoods. We crossed the Colorado on an old suspension bridge. Here in the heart of the canyon spread a bustling complex, the Phantom Ranch cabins, ranger quarters, the park campground and helipad, even a sewage treatment plant from which solid waste, after treatment, is packed out by mule. We heard talk of a mule going over the edge at Panorama Point. It was a fatal misstep, I learned later, taken by a pack mule, not one that carried riders. After some debate over what to do with the victim, it was decided to let nature take its course—but to move the animal downslope some distance to avoid a pan-aroma round Panorama. "We haven't had a life-and-death accident with a rider in my ten years here. This is the safest transportation in the world," said livery manager Ron Clayton of the Fred Harvey Company, the South Rim concessionaire.

The spread at Phantom Ranch seemed quite elaborate to me. I favor the purist attitude toward amenities in the backcountry. Less is more; the comforts of home diminish the wilderness. But I must confess that nothing in any national park, wild or tame, ever gave me more pleasure than the amenity of the telephone message waiting at the ranch. Back East, a few hours earlier, Alexander Jeffrey Fishbein had arrived. Grand child, grand news, Grand Canyon.

Here, too, I had the pleasure of spending some time with Sjors. He has a last name but doesn't use it much. Doesn't need to. Netherlands-born and now in his mid-30s, Sjors was a television repairman in Los Angeles. He did not like it out there. He loves it down here. He patrols the campground and trails, cleaning up, revegetating trampled areas, helping rangers with medical emergencies—for five dollars a day and a place to stay, without board. This is the pay for a park volunteer, when there's money to pay it. From all I heard about Sjors, we taxpayers are getting a sensational bargain.

For Sjors it's enough, supplemented by dinner invitations at the ranch and by food from campers eager to lighten their packs before heading up the canyon. Sjors is not one of those marginal souls eddied out of the mainstream and marking time until they can manage a reentry. For him the bottom of the canyon is liberation, a base for trips to splendid crannies where the amenities are solitude, hidden cataracts, rainbows in the rock, and a thin blue line of sky.

A half dozen or more kinds of scorpions inhabit the canyon; one of them—the slender scorpion—can kill humans. The others can hurt. A ranger formerly stationed at Phantom Ranch told me she had been stung on an arm there one summer. She remembered the aftermath as the most excruciating 18 hours of her life: "My veins felt like they were exploding. When a fly landed on my arm, it felt like an elephant." Some residents of the canyon depths, I've heard, plant their bed legs in glass jars to dissuade scorpions from climbing up into bed. Sjors has his own way: "I just catch them and feed them a fly. And the next day I let them loose. I call it good scorpion karma. And they leave me alone."

Sjors hikes all over the canyon, but rarely out of it. "I feel at home here," he told me. "It's very friendly, but it's also a very wild place. I think that's mainly it. It's free. There are very few places where you can feel free. If I ever leave, it will probably be to go to another canyon."

"I feel at home here. It's very friendly, but it's also a very wild place. I think that's mainly it. It's free. There are very few places where you can feel free."

My companions and I sprawled into a campsite shaded by cottonwoods and hedged with willows beside the creek. After such a hike, I thought, there is no shade more refreshing than the shade of these cottonwoods, no lullaby more soothing than the lullaby of the Bright Angel tumbling through the soaring side canyon. I soon drowsed off.

As the day cooled, we hiked a mile or two up the Clear Creek Trail to watch the sun fade along the river and the inner gorge, the towers of black and red rock turning gloomy and gothic with nightfall. Scarcely a thousand feet high, the jagged inner gorge walls, so unlike the layered sequence above, are the roots of mountains, which, about two billion years ago, rose several miles higher than they do now. Heat and pressure altered, or metamorphosed, the rock into schist; slowly cooling magma intruded from below, blending red granite into the dark schist. Erosion wore the great range down to a plain. The rocky plain was submerged beneath a shallow sea that began to form the first of many layers of sediment upon the schist. The earliest of those layers—the billion-year-old Bass limestone—contains stromatolites, mats of fossil algae, the first evidence of life in the canyon.

The cool evening hours lure others out on the trail. Had Bill Breed not recognized the sound of the rattle, we might have stepped on it, a pink Grand Canyon rattlesnake about two feet long. Under the flashlight beam it backed off, and we backed off, and stepped very, very carefully all the way back to camp.

Next day Bill and I hiked up Phantom Canyon, which feeds into Bright Angel, a tight little side canyon of a side canyon. Phantom was a delightful boulder scramble, with frequent crossings of a creek edged with willows and cattails and dotted with patriarchal cottonwoods. There was box elder and monkeyflower and fleabane in bloom. There was a water ouzel dipping, and a good breeze, and we went on, following each curve, till the walls pinched in so that we could straddle the creek, each foot against opposite canyon walls. And here in the shade, we rested in reverie. "Canyons are like peanuts," Bill laughed. "You can't stop with one look. You've always got to see what's around the next bend."

*H*ere in the shade, we rested in reverie. "Canyons are like peanuts," Bill laughed. "You can't stop with one look. You've always got to see what's around the next bend."

Sometimes you go too far, on days when canyons are not all that idyllic. On a 110-degree day in 1985 park interpreter Dale Schmidt and his girlfriend Katy, a park ranger, decided to cool off in a lake formed by a rockslide in Phantom Canyon, far beyond where Bill and I turned back. In late morning Katy headed back to work; Dale hiked up the canyon, found a boulder above the creek, and took a nap. He woke to a low rumbling. "I looked up and saw a muddy wall of water coming at me. I went up the cliff as fast as I could, and when I looked down, there was a 12-foot wall of water that had taken my pack. When I hiked down, I never found the lake; the flash flood tore the rockslide out and the lake drained away." Katy had hiked out before the deluge, and when she returned to the mouth of the creek and saw the path of the flood, hope for Dale drained away. "He was my best boyfriend, and now he's gone," she called on the park radio. He emerged spattered with mud. Later, on a happier day in Phantom Canyon, Dale proposed. Katy is now Katy Schmidt.

Night in the campground brings a sense of containment, of solid, encircling walls. Gradually the focus narrows to a starlit wedge of sky. Then the canyon sucks in some wind. Cool gusts snap by, and the pliant cottonwood crowns brush across the starlight. The air is wine, the creek and wind rush, a symphony. Many, many a night have I cursed a stubborn insomnia. Not now. On this sweet desert night, sleep is a waste.

Higher and wetter, and thus more heavily eroded, the North Rim lies farther back from the river than does the South Rim. The North Kaibab Trail stretches more than 14 miles, twice as long as the South Kaibab. It begins as a gentle upward tug boxed by shadowy walls beside frolicking Bright Angel Creek, which has cut down through its namesake fault. Grasses and leafy trees edge the waters; cactuses dot rock walls that ring with the loud, descending whistle of the troubadour of the gorge, the canyon wren. The boring house wrens in my backyard could learn a trill or two here.

So went the morning hours as we began the long leg of the rim-to-rim trek. And when the sun caught up to us, the side trail to Ribbon Falls lay just ahead. A short hike brought us to the falls. Working around its mossy dome of travertine, the cascade of maidenhair fern, and the clusters of red monkeyflowers, we found a spray-cooled dining alcove behind the falls. Then we stripped and, shivering and bellowing, took the cold, hard gush head on, then resumed our hike, refreshed. At Cottonwood Camp, seven miles from our start, we refilled the water bottles and ate some more. People addicted to frequent snacking have found their heaven in Grand Canyon country. This is a nosher's paradise. The rule of canyon hiking is that of a doting mother: Eat, eat, eat, have a little more, peanuts, raisins, cookies. You call it junk food? Nah. Good for you. The trail burns it up. Only one little problem. First you have to carry it all on your back.

A hot mile and a half beyond Cottonwood a touch of suburbia appears directly ahead, like a mirage: a brown frame house, vines on the veranda, box elders, picket fence, green lawn, a vegetable garden. This is the home of Bruce Aiken, another city boy who found a life in the heart of Grand Canyon. We had met a few times on the South Rim and hoped to meet again here. But a conflict arose. Bruce's daughters, Mercy and Shirley, had leading parts in a high school play. Bruce wouldn't—couldn't—dare miss it. So he hiked 5½ miles to the North Rim, drove 215 miles to the South Rim school. Next day he would backtrack the route to resume what he calls his "babysitting" at the Roaring Springs pump house, a mile above his home.

Bruce Aiken grew up in Greenwich Village and studied at a Manhattan art school. "I was painting landscapes out of my head," he recalled. "They said, 'That's crazy, you should be doing abstract expressionism.' When I was 20, I came out here on a lark, and I took one look around and I said, 'Hey, wait a minute, I thought I was making this up.' " He heard of an opening at the pump house in the early '70s. "I cut my hair real short, bought some Levi's, and convinced them I could do the job. When the man who hired me saw me pick up a wrench, he looked kind of funny, though." The job is simple, Bruce says, just a daily check of the station and maintenance of the equipment that pumps water out of Roaring Springs to the North Rim. Occasionally he checks for breaks in the pipeline that carries the water up. Another pipe carries water by gravity down to Phantom Ranch, across the Colorado, and up to Indian Gardens, whence it is pumped to the South Rim, the sole water source for nearly four million visitors.

Bruce and Mary Aiken raised Mercy, Shirley, and their son, Silas, in the canyon depths, teaching them at home until the abstractions of algebra stumped them. And Bruce painted—the rich colors and textures of the rock, the high temples and the shadowed depths, the waterfalls and the flowers. He has shown in galleries from coast to coast, sold paintings in the five figures—and never got around to abstract expressionism.

At Roaring Springs the trail turns away from Bright Angel and heads northwest up Roaring Springs Canyon: piñon and juniper, hop hornbeam and manzanita shrub, and the cruel splendor of the Redwall. Sunshine washes pinnacles, buttresses, hanging ledges. Smoldering red walls await the spark of sunlight. Only birdsong and the muffled roar of the spring behind us break the silence. A dark gray spire called the Needle rises out of the canyon; standing alone, unstained by the red rocks, it shows the true color of the Redwall limestone. Higher up lies one of the springtime treats of the canyon, redbud in bloom.

Three or four hikers catch us from behind and move ahead briskly. Whoa, wait, what's the hurry? Jim von Dorn, a systems analyst in Phoenix, explains. He and his friends left the South Rim, some 19 miles ago, at 2:30 this morning. Before this day is done they will touch the North Rim and double back—rim to rim to rim, 42 miles—in less than 18 hours. "Kind of a personal challenge," Jim replies to the obvious query. "Gets us out of the office."

We have done a fraction of that this day, and when I look behind, down the narrow chute, even that puny stretch doesn't look doable. But it was.

Before long we top out, into the high forest world of the North Rim, cooling off in a shadowed bank of grimy snow. Here, too, as on the South Rim, hundreds of millions of years of earth history and thousands of feet of rock have eroded away. Thank heavens.

*L*ike *a black thread, the 440-foot-long Kaibab Bridge stitches the canyon. It, and the Silver Bridge beyond, hang from rock 1.7 billion years old. FOLLOWING PAGES: Solid floor of the Kaibab Bridge keeps mules from viewing the river.*

GARY LADD; DAVID HISER (FOLLOWING PAGES)

Diamondlike cascade of Ribbon Falls cools a side canyon along the North Rim's Kaibab Trail. Trail-dusty visitors climb up to refresh themselves in the icy spray. Travertine, composed of calcium carbonate deposited by the splashing water, forms an apron at the base of the falls. Below, a Grand Canyon rattler blends with the shading of its red-rock surroundings; this subspecies lives only in the giant gorge.

DAVID HISER

ANIMALS ANIMALS / ZIG LESZCZYNSKI

101

*C*anyon contrast: Delicate flowers of
a globemallow bloom beside inch-long
spines of an Engelmann's prickly pear
(opposite). Herb and cactus, common
in the canyon, have adapted to aridity.
Prickly pears grow to four feet here.
One clings to Redwall on the North
Kaibab Trail, where geologist William
Breed points out color variations
in the limestone to the author.

DAVID HISER; ©LARRY ULRICH (OPPOSITE)

JEFF GNASS

*R*esident and wayfarer: A great horned owl glares from a sandstone perch as a hiker heads down the North Kaibab Trail below Komo Point on the North Rim.

FOLLOWING PAGES: The North Kaibab winds up to the rim past Douglas firs nourished by rain and snowmelt.

TOM BEAN; DAVID HISER (FOLLOWING PAGES)

North Rim
Country

*V*iew *from the top: Fingers of cloud and rock
interlace below Point Imperial, at 8,803 feet the
highest overlook on either rim of the Grand Canyon.*

DICK DIETRICH; ©PAT O'HARA (PRECEDING PAGES)

*T*wisted piñon pine crowns a view from Walhalla Plateau, easternmost segment
of the North Rim—the higher, cooler, wetter, and more eroded side of the canyon.

W hite-haired, his face as seamed and tan as a walnut, Mickey Segmiller kept a running dialogue with the bawling cattle that we had gathered out of the hot, dry flats of House Rock Valley. "Hee-YAH, hee-YAH, git along, git along, git along," he urged them. Mel Heaton whistled while he worked them. "J. R." Jones encouraged the laggards with a soft flick of his "hard twist," which is what the old-timers call a lariat here on the Arizona Strip.

The pregnant cows have wintered here, and some have already dropped their calves. It is only April, way too early to be driving cattle from winter range, and yet Dave Johnson has his cowboys out, rousting the cows, moving them around. "They're grubbing the range," Dave explains. "The feed's all gone, and we didn't get any regrowth last year. We're just juggling pastures, trying to keep 'em from beating out any one too badly. We were raised on this land, and we try hard to take good care of it."

So we drift the cows from nibbled-out patches to others, where the four-winged saltbush and the sage and the Mormon tea and the grasses are a little greener. To my eye there's not a whole lot to choose from. This is high desert in a dry season in a run of dry years, government-owned grazing land stretching to the western edge of Marble Canyon.

Except around the water holes, the animals are spread thin. It takes a lot of land to feed a cow here. The government permits, Dave tells me, allow about three cows to graze a square mile. Even fewer can graze on the west side of the Strip, toward the Nevada border. During one stretch of drought out there, rancher Duane Blake told me later, "I went seven years without a profit." He holds permits on various sections. One group of permits for 15 sections allows him to winter 40 cows—40 cows on 15 square miles.

It took little more than a century for government regulation to spread across the ranges where pioneering ranchers bought springs from Native Americans for a horse or rifle, purchased seeps for a blanket, and grazed herds, which, by the late 1800s, numbered cattle in the tens of thousands, sheep in the hundreds of thousands. Drought and overgrazing scarred the Strip. Today, even two or three cows to the square mile are too many for some in the environmentalist

Sinuous, sheer-walled Paria Canyon dwarfs not only hikers but also the river that sculptured it—the Paria. The chasm lies within Paria Canyon–Vermilion Cliffs Wilderness Area, overseen by the Bureau of Land Management.

GARY LADD

community who oppose grazing generally as a threat to the fragility and the harsh beauty of publicly owned desert lands. One hears the rallying cry often out West: "No moo in '92."

Once a herd gets bunched and is moving forward steadily, Mickey and Mel and J. R. tend to ride behind it, pulling out as needed to push along little mavericks caterwauling on the fringes. I, too, ride the fringes, occasionally exchanging sullen glances with a would-be stray before it lopes off to join the crowd. Often I stare at the cowboys, envying their effortless saddle sway. What is the secret to it? My mount, Navajo, is a gentle 12-year-old sorrel, no quirks at all. Yet he immediately senses that I am a novice, so I am constantly "pulling leather," clinging to the saddle horn to deploy arms and shoulders as auxiliary shock absorbers. Body and spirit hurt. The cowboys had balm—for the spirit, at least. They recalled for me the invincible TV lawman, a long-running legend of the tube, who outrode, outpunched, and outdrew the orneriest polecats in the wild, wild West. His exploits were filmed around Kanab, just above the Utah border. What didn't appear in the weekly escapade was the apple crate the marshall stepped on each time he mounted up. "I carried that apple box a long ways for him," laughed Dave Johnson. That was soothing; nobody's perfect.

Our range lay on the easternmost of a series of plateaus that make up the "Lonesome Country," the "North of the River Country"—better known today as the Arizona Strip. Set off from Utah by the state boundary and cut off from the rest of Arizona by the Grand Canyon, the Strip covers 8,400 square miles. You can tuck Connecticut, Delaware, and Rhode Island into it with a hundred square miles to spare. You can count its towns on one hand with fingers to spare. In 1949 local historian Juanita Brooks described it as "the essence of space and silence, where the land sprawls and stretches and breathes deeply beneath the sun, rousing to a brief blossoming in the spring, to drop again into somnolence." Over the years people who had a good reason to hide found it a good place to hide. Today tens of thousands tour it, hike it, ski it, hunt it, ranch it, log it, and mine it.

Only a tiny fraction of the Arizona Strip—239 square miles—is privately owned. The Kaibab Indian Reservation covers 189 square miles. The rest is government land—Grand Canyon National Park, Lake Mead National Recreation Area, Kaibab National Forest, and holdings of the Bureau of Land Management (BLM) and the state of Arizona. Conservation struggles have brought wilderness protection to fine swaths of national forest and BLM land—including Kanab Creek and its spectacular canyon, the landmark Saddle Mountain, the Beaver Dam Mountains, and the Grand Wash Cliffs over on the west. From House Rock we can see the brilliant edge of the Paria Canyon–Vermilion Cliffs Wilderness Area, a 3,000-foot escarpment of many shades and moods. When the light strikes the red rock just so, I think: "Prime rib, extremely rare." The cliffs look raw and barren, but there are precious springs in them; from the springs miles and miles of pipe descend to water game and grazing stock. In 1984 the Paria Canyon and

Vermilion Cliffs areas were combined to form one long, nearly circular wilderness that covers 110,000 acres. Wilderness preservation did not end the battle for the land; it goes on—over logging, grazing, uranium mining, park development.

To the west and north of where we ride in sweat and dust rises the cool forest highland that welcomes hikers emerging from the abyss. Still snowflecked on its flanks, it is a long plateau running north and south, the highest reach of a geologic upheaval where the Grand Canyon has made its most dramatic cut. To Larry Stevens, author of *The Colorado River in Grand Canyon*, a reference guide for river runners, the plateau resembles "a loaf of bread resting on a table." The Southern Paiute, who hunted deer across the height, called it Kaibab—"Mountain Lying Down." The more I roamed the backcountry north of the Colorado—on foot, on horseback, on skis, and in four-wheel drives—the more I concurred with Clarence Dutton's judgment: "The other plateaus are formidable deserts; the Kaibab is a paradise." It is where the cows will go in June.

---

*T*he more I roamed the backcountry north of the Colorado . . . the more I concurred with Clarence Dutton's judgment: "The other plateaus are formidable deserts; the Kaibab is a paradise."

Here in the North of the River Country, Dutton's eloquence reached the sublime. Here on a remote canyon shelf spreads a gallery of the most striking prehistoric rock art yet discovered in the national park. Here frozen lava chokes side canyons near volcanic mountains where Mormons—members of the Church of Jesus Christ of Latter-day Saints—harvested stately timbers for a temple meant to last until the millennium. Here Teddy Roosevelt enjoyed great sport, riding with hounds to tree mountain lions—"the big horse-killing cat, the destroyer of the deer, the lord of stealthy murder, facing his doom with a heart both craven and cruel." Thus, in foamy, telepathic prose, T. R. read the heart of the beast at the climax of the hunt—as "the maddened hounds bayed" and a rifle shot delivered death.

Some years earlier, President Roosevelt had established the Grand Canyon Game Reserve, providing total protection for deer and unleashing a campaign of extermination against predators such as the mountain lion. Roosevelt hunted with the most illustrious of the campaigners, James T. "Uncle Jim" Owens. Warden of the reserve, Owens killed some 500 cougars, covered his cabin walls with lion claws, and offered "Lions Caught to Order, Reasonable Rates." One of his captives was packed across the canyon on horseback, and for a time was on display at the El Tovar Hotel on the South Rim.

Lion-chasing here lured a New York dentist born Pearl Zane Gray, renamed Zane Grey, who aspired to a literary career. The cougars and the canyon colors, the cowboys and the Indians, the deserts and the mustangs and the hardy Mormon frontiersmen—canyon country inspired a gush of western tales that made Zane Grey world famous, as well as the Hollywood cowboys who starred in the movie versions of his stories.

---

*A*t day's end—or long after, in black night
when all we could see were the sparks of hoofs
clattering on Kaibab limestone—the cowboys turned
the horses into a corral with century-old timbers. . . .

History lives here, in lonely landmarks and in tales told by lamplight. At day's end—or long after, in black night when all we could see were the sparks of hoofs clattering on Kaibab limestone—the cowboys turned the horses into a corral with century-old timbers and gathered in a house with century-old stone siding at the Kane Ranch. As we rested on the porch, an enormous moon bounced up from the Echo Cliffs beyond Marble Canyon, turning from gold to silver as it floated upward and shrank. Wow! said I, in a verbal swoon. The cowboys took it calmly. Happens every month, said one.

Mel Heaton, steeped in Strip history, and Dave Johnson told of the conflict that brought Mormon ranchers to this lonely sagebrush flat. In 1887 continuing national pressure on the Mormons to stop their practice of plural marriage produced the Edmunds-Tucker, or Anti-Polygamy, Act; it declared all church property forfeit to the government. One of the threatened properties was a tithing herd—cattle tithed to the Mormon Church by members—at Pipe Springs, some 50 miles to the northwest, near the town of Moccasin, Arizona. (Dave and Mel live in Moccasin, surrounded by the Paiute's Kaibab Reservation, where Mickey Segmiller lives.) The church transferred title to the herd to a company headed by

116

John Young, Mormon elder Brigham Young's son, and the animals were driven to House Rock. Later, famous Arizona Strip outfits such as the Bar Z of the Grand Canyon Cattle Company operated here. Finally, the Kane Ranch property and grazing permits for hundreds of thousands of acres were bought by Emil "E. J." Graff, a wealthy merchant, farmer, and rancher of Hurricane, Utah.

Dave manages the Graff outfit. A few days before I joined the cowpunchers at House Rock, E. J. died at the age of 97. He left about half of the Kane Ranch operation to the church, according to his son Shirl, a Salt Lake City physician. "Dad told me he had hoped that the property could be saved for a hundred years or until the Second Coming, so that when Jesus returned, He would have enough money to do what He had to do."

By propane lantern light Dave's father, 73-year-old Owen Johnson, recalled the days when his father, uncles, and grandfather operated Lees Ferry, the historic Colorado River crossing, now the busy put-in for river runners. The crossing was often dangerous and sometimes fatal. Young Owen was living there in the late 1920s when a spring torrent tore the ferry loose, drowning a cousin and two other men. By that time construction crews—including Johnson men— were at work a few miles downstream on the Navajo Bridge. The ferry was never replaced. Today the bridge carries traffic of Route 89A, the only highway across the eastern reaches of the Strip.

"When I started cowpunching," Owen recalled, "I got a dollar a day and board. When it came to two dollars a day, I thought I'd reached the top." Cowboy wages remain unglamorous. Most of the men I rode with love the tradition but must do other things to make ends meet. Dave Johnson still cowboys full time, vanning his riding stock out to the ranges—he has put 60,000 miles on a year-old pickup—and then spending more hours in the saddle each day working the stock. "For young people these days," he reflected, "there are easier ways to make a living than for those of us who grew up knowing nothing else."

Some 12 miles of dirt road south from the Kane Ranch, I spent a lively hour with Chic Wayne, Arizona game warden at the 60,000-acre House Rock Buffalo Ranch. The historic bison herd that roams this range is the legacy of Charles Jesse "Buffalo" Jones, a wildlife manipulator of international celebrity. He had joined in the great buffalo slaughter, then tried to preserve the remnants; he caught cougars with a lasso; in Yellowstone he trapped delinquent grizzlies and spanked them. For Zane Grey he was mentor and inspiration, hero of *The Last of the Plainsmen*. During the administration of his friend and fellow conservationist, President Theodore Roosevelt, Jones received a permit to run bison on the Kaibab Plateau. And he pursued his dream of breeding buffalo bulls to domestic cows. The animals preferred the open land of House Rock Valley to the forest. Jones's "cattalo" scheme foundered amid the complexities and mortality of the crossbreeding experiments. "Uncle Jim" Owens of cougar-hunting fame inherited part of the bison herd from Jones and sold it to the Arizona State Game and Fish Commission in 1926.

Chic Wayne keeps an eye on the descendants and on the pipe-fed water tanks that make this range habitable for them. Right now the buffalo were out of sight, some ten miles away munching grasses and cliff roses on the lower slopes of Saddle Mountain. They totaled 120; with the help of licensed hunters Arizona aimed for a herd of 90.

"It isn't much of a hunt, is it?" I asked, reflecting the conventional wisdom about these huge, standstill targets.

Chic guffawed. "If you go at it like that, I'll guarantee you wouldn't get one. Probably you're not smart enough, you're not strong enough, you can't hold up long enough to get one. You probably wouldn't ever see a buffalo.

"If you go at it like that, I'll guarantee you wouldn't get one. Probably you're not smart enough, you're not strong enough, you can't hold up long enough to get one."

"As a casual visitor when they're not being hunted, you may not appreciate what a buffalo is. But when you start hunting him, he's real skilled at staying away. He gets down behind a bush, and he's hid. If you don't put out a lot of effort and you're looking at a hundred square miles of country, you won't find him. In this country they can outrun good, tough trucks. They give you a heck of a hunt.

"Once I watched a herd of about a hundred right out here in the open. Something like 20 hunters surrounded the herd at daylight. You'd have thought it would be a slaughter. But the leader cow didn't stampede and run off cross-country. She started playing checkers, run a little ways, then see what position the hunters took. And I watched her maneuver that whole herd through those people and escape with only two buffalo lost."

With T. R.'s establishment of the Grand Canyon Game Reserve in 1906, friends of the mule deer on the Kaibab Plateau had sought to provide a refuge free of enemies—hunters banned, predators destroyed or removed. Livestock grazing was severely cut back; the deer had free run and multiplied. By the 1920s, it could be said, the Kaibab deer herd needed enemies, not friends. The herd had erupted from 4,000 to several times that number. Estimates of the new total varied from 30,000 to 100,000, modern studies tending toward the lower figure. Whatever the total, the deer were starving on a blasted range.

In 1924 someone in Flagstaff got the idea of driving thousands of Kaibab deer from South Canyon to Saddle Mountain, and down rugged Nankoweap Canyon to the bottom of the Grand Canyon; the animals would swim across the Colorado River, climb up the Tanner Trail to the South Rim, and move to a new home on a range shy of deer. The scheme needed money. Zane Grey, by then a world-famed author with movie interests, rode to the rescue. For exclusive literary and film rights to the drive, Grey and his partners provided backing.

One cold day in December about 130 men strung out in a line, on foot and on horseback, armed with cowbells and tin cans. "With a crash that sounded like an aborted clap of thunder," wrote John P. Russo in his history of the Kaibab herd, "the line moved forward, men hollering and clanging their noise makers." The deer seemed unfazed by the noise, but the herding tactics of the horsemen touched off a stampede. The terrified deer fled every way but straight ahead. At one point Grey reached for his gun as his horse gave way before a charging buck. Darkness fell, and the next morning, snow. Men got lost in the storm. When the drive was abandoned, there were thousands of deer behind the men, but none in front. Grey wrote a short piece for the *Coconino Sun,* a Flagstaff paper, blaming "inadequate preparation, lack of enough drivers and the total unexpected refusal of the deer to herd." He ended with a little sermon on the balance of nature, recalling that he and Buffalo Jones, "some 15 years ago, advised the government not to kill off the cougars" and noting "how futile it is for men to interfere with the laws of nature."

The killing went on, however, even as the deer dropped dead from starvation, and the government created "fawn farms" to bottle-nurse young deer on cow's milk until they could be sold and shipped off. Today the cougar, officially removed from the bounty list only in 1990, and the mule deer are both hunted. The Arizona Game and Fish Department manages the deer herd, while the Kaibab National Forest manages the habitat. In the fall of 1990 Arizona game officials put the deer numbers at 28,000, offered 8,050 hunting permits, and anticipated a kill of 3,700. Logging continues on the national forest, including the game reserve. Kaibab National Forest biologist Keith Menasco insists that deer habitat has actually been enhanced by carefully planned timber harvesting.

At my favorite Flagstaff café, where I frequently feasted on sprouts, meatless hamburgers, and white wine, I pursued the timber issue one day in the gentle, cooing discourse we environmentalists dote on. "It's a national disgrace," said Sharon Galbreath, chairperson of the Sierra Club's Plateau Group. "All the guidelines they've set for protection of spotted owls, goshawks, Kaibab squirrels, wild turkeys, and deer can't be met with the volume they've promised the timber industry."

In an executive summary published in February 1990, the state game and fish department expressed "a rapidly growing concern over conflicts between management of wildlife and its habitat and the ever-increasing emphasis on timber production on the state's national forests." Keith Menasco acknowledges that concern; Forest Service officials have ordered a "re-analysis" of timber output and an interim reduction of the 1991 harvest from 61 to 50 million board feet.

After wrestling "mightily with the Lord," the beleaguered leader of the Mormon Church in 1890 officially proclaimed polygamy at an end. Church property was returned; Utah won statehood in 1896. The Mormon Church excommunicates those who practice plural marriage. Though not widespread, it does persist. It lives on today at the northern edge of the Arizona Strip, hard by the Utah border, in Colorado City, a quiet community of spacious houses, clean-shaven men with conservative haircuts, and modestly dressed women.

In the office of elementary school principal Warren Johnson, I spoke to his father, Orval, a first cousin of Owen Johnson of Moccasin. "My father," said Orval, "was born at Lees Ferry. His father had two wives. When the church stopped living plural marriage, grandfather refused to say to one of them, 'Wife, you go 'way. I won't have anything more to do with you.' He kept his two wives. We have a very strong belief in this. It never changed with father. It was part of his innermost feelings. Like begets like, I suppose."

In the 1930s, like-minded believers in the old ways formed the community of Colorado City, known then as Short Creek. The city is a refuge for a splinter group that split from the Mormon Church after it abandoned polygamy. The site, I had heard, had the usual virtues of an Arizona Strip address—beyond the reach of Utah law, too remote from Arizona law for anyone to bother. Orval demurred, vigorously. There were raids in the '30s, harassment in the '40s, and, in 1953, a full-scale roundup. Arizona authorities arrested 26 men and carried away 253 children to be placed in foster homes. "I was breaking no law," said Orval. "I had one wife and five children. They took my children because I resided here in this community where we believe Mormonism. They took our people and scattered them all over the state." Orval pointed to a gray-haired school aide at a nearby filing cabinet. "Marjorie Holm had (Continued on page 133)

*B*alancing boulders, remnants
of harder Shinarump rock survive
atop pedestals of relatively soft
Moenkopi stone near Lees Ferry.
FOLLOWING PAGES: Westering sun
ignites aptly named Vermilion Cliffs.

JACK W. DYKINGA (OPPOSITE AND FOLLOWING PAGES)

120

Silver-skinned aspen trees—almost nonexistent on the dry South Rim— border grassy flats of Greenland Lake (left) on Walhalla Plateau. Mud and vegetation slow drainage enough to leave standing water here. The North Rim receives up to 30 inches of rain and 10 feet of snow yearly, but water seeps into the porous limestone. Introduced in 1949, wild turkeys, like the one below, thrive on the cool North Rim.

DICK DIETRICH

ERWIN & PEGGY BAUER

125

ERWIN & PEGGY BAUER

*F*urrowed brow of a cougar seems to mirror conservationists' concerns for its future. Canyon natives decimated by bounty hunters, the cats are legal game outside the park.

*B*adlands incarnate: Tortuous, deeply gouged rockscapes dominate the scene from Kanab Point (right). Greater rainfall and faster uplift has left the North Rim more dissected than the South. At Toroweap Overlook (below) less than one mile separates the canyon rims; tourists watch the Colorado River churning 3,000 feet directly below them.

DANNY LEHMAN

TOM TILL

DAVID HISER (BOTH)

*H*eavy cowhide chaps protect the skin but not the muscles of Mickey Segmiller (opposite) as he begins another day driving cattle to new pasture on the Arizona Strip (above). Recent drought years and 19th-century overgrazing depleted the Strip's range. Some environmental groups oppose continued grazing on this dry public domain.

a little girl in 1953 who was quite delicate in nature. She got ill, and they took her off the bus in Flagstaff, took her to a hospital and she died—because of that raid." Orval got his children back and, in the fullness of time, was blessed with a total of 44—of whom, he says proudly, only one was lost to the fundamentalist beliefs of the community.

Some weeks later, chatting with former Arizona Governor Bruce Babbitt on a steamy day deep in the Grand Canyon, I mentioned Colorado City's bitter memories of the 1953 raid. Babbitt regards it as a shameful moment in his state's history. "When I took office in 1978," he told me, "I felt I had to make amends. I visited them and was coolly received. But I found the school was a special need and arranged to help them build an addition." There were pressures on the governor to crack down on the polygamous town. Babbitt resisted. "Arizona had much higher priorities in crime to deal with," he said.

South of Colorado City and west of the Mountain Lying Down, there are places worthy of the encomium penned by a traveler passing through the Strip: "All the bad country in the U.S. was put together and they called it Arizona." Early in the century Sharlot Hall, historian of Arizona Territory, described "roads that would tire an eagle to fly over." Those roads still wind across the space and silence of the Strip. Here lie sprawling tracts of Bureau of Land Management wilderness where no motorized vehicle may travel and faint ruts, edging the very lip of the Grand Canyon, along which, as Dennis Curtis of the BLM likes to say, "you can have a wilderness experience without getting out of your vehicle." And here stretches acre after acre where one may learn yet again that "bad" country is not the same as ugly country.

To prove the truth of his words, Dennis drove me to some of those bring-water-camp-anywhere places, and to abandoned mines and to lonely ranches so dry that people collect and reuse water to tend their orchards and their stock. Homesteaders in the area were known locally as dry-nesters or dry-farmers because of the lack of water on their lands.

We drove out of St. George, the hub of Utah's "Dixie" and northwestern Arizona, south across the state border on an unpaved thoroughfare of the Shivwits

Flame-tipped Indian paintbrush
blaze among sprigs of purple lupine,
a legume that helps fertilize the soil.
Wildflowers of every hue grace the
North Rim, which boasts the canyon's
most diverse ecology and topography.

INGE MARTIN

Plateau, down Wolf Hole Valley and into Main Street Valley. In bygone days— when the Strip was "sheeped to death"—the lamps and campfires of sheepherders seemed to string through the valley like the lights of Main Street.

We drove through Hurricane Valley, where homesteaders tried dry-land farming until the dry land starved them out. We skirted Poverty Mountain and stopped to trade greetings with Buster Esplin, who was currying his horses near his green rambler home. A lonely life, I thought. How long does it take to get to town? "Oh," Buster laughed, "three to eight hours, depending on who I meet." We headed on south to the Parashant country and ate lunch ten feet from Grand Canyon National Park. We looked down on the broad Sanup Plateau; to the west we could see the Colorado fanning out into Lake Mead, the impoundment of Hoover Dam.

"Anywhere along here," said Dennis, "you can find views like these and play the roads for hours without seeing anyone." We ground slowly into Snap Canyon and onto the bench between two lines of the Grand Wash Cliffs to the Grand Gulch copper mine—a ghostly array of rusting trucks, hollow shells of buildings, a tall smelter chimney. Miners had bought the site from Indians for some flour and a horse.

Down the Virgin River Gorge we drove, between the Beaver Dam and the Paiute Wildernesses, the road edged with creosote bushes in yellow bloom and the hillsides studded with Joshua trees flaunting their creamy blossoms. Pink flowers glowed in the beavertail cactus. We were on the northern edge of the Mojave Desert, in the border region between the Colorado Plateau and the Great Basin. We dipped down into Nevada, the desert now abloom with glittery resorts and billboards.

On the Beaver Dam Slope we beheld BLM biologist Tim Duck in a Statue of Liberty pose, holding high an antenna to home in on a desert tortoise. Soon the squeaky radio signals brought the target into view, an inert, ten-inch oval resting amid creosote and bursage. An old highway, once the artery between Las Vegas and Salt Lake City, runs close by the Beaver Dam Slope; gas stations there used to give away a desert tortoise with each fill-up. Now it is the threatened desert tortoise, here glued to a radio pack in the struggle for survival.

Ranchers hereabouts have been sending their own signals about the desert tortoise. What galls some, especially, is a new BLM program that invites tourists onto scenic byways through the heart of sensitive tortoise habitat. Most ranchers fear the prospect of new restrictions on grazing in desert terrain where they are already restricted to fewer than three cows to the square mile.

"There's some dietary overlap between cattle and tortoises in the springtime," said Tim, "and some instances when a concentration of cattle may cause problems. But the standard notion of a cow stepping on a tortoise and crushing it or ripping the food out of a tortoise's mouth is really sensationalism. There are people who emotionally don't want cattle grazing in the desert, so they've made some claims that have never been justified."

134

In the springtime the tortoises awake from their winter dormancy to feast nonstop on tender new grasses. During summer's heat they hole up in their burrows. In the fall monsoon storms crackle. Then, said Tim, "the tortoises come out to fill their canteens, storing as much as a third of their body weight in water. And they'll draw on that to help digest the grasses that have turned to straw. They may void their bladder only once a year, maybe twice if they get a good early spring rain."

The Kaibab Plateau . . . "is covered with a beautiful forest, and in the forest charming parks are found. . . . the plateau has four months of the sweetest summer man has ever known."

The Kaibab Plateau, wrote John Wesley Powell, "is covered with a beautiful forest, and in the forest charming parks are found. . . . In winter deep snows lie here, but the plateau has four months of the sweetest summer man has ever known." Mormon ranchers summered their cattle in the extensive meadows of one of those charming parks. In 1911, according to Sharlot Hall, it was "a narrow, almost level valley running for seven miles between low hills, thickly forested with spruce." It was often called V. T. Park. V. T. may stand for Valley Tan, an epithet with interesting associations in Mormon lore. According to author Wallace Stegner, the term originally stood for cheap leather, then for anything crudely made, especially a vile form of rotgut dubbed "leopard sweat." The park is now called DeMotte, after professor Harvey C. DeMotte, who explored the Kaibab Plateau and the North Rim of the canyon with Major Powell in the summer of 1872.

For a few January days, while the snows still lay deep, I skied DeMotte, a narrow, treeless flat hemmed by spruce-clad hills. The open grassland, reminiscent of the big-sky swards of the northern Rockies, once served as a summer headquarters for Kane Ranch cowboys.

A concessionaire's ski van picked up a group of us at Jacob Lake and ground slowly along logging roads for 26 miles, slowly enough for us to enjoy the stands of aspen, study the bronzy, deeply grooved bark of the soaring ponderosa pines, and bemoan the clear-cut patches. We got off at a summer store

135

turned winter camp, the gas pumps all but buried in the snow. DeMotte Park glittered under brilliant sunshine; despite the frosty white expanse, this is still the Sun Belt.

Our skills varied widely. Dixie Green of Kanab, Utah, had never been on cross-country skis before. She has one degree in bacteriology and another in accounting, has worked in the South and on the West Coast, and has sought to make life an adventure. And though she has come home to her roots in Utah, her quest has not ended. Dixie took her first Nordic lesson from me, poor soul. Despite this handicap, she decided on the morning after our arrival to join the six-mile trek to East Rim Viewpoint.

The little knoll that edged the east side of the park became a bear of a hill on skis. It got the sweat flowing, and the sunshine kept it flowing, even when the terrain flattened out. East Rim Viewpoint, at the edge of Saddle Mountain Wilderness, spread a fine panorama of House Rock Valley before us. Across the valley ran the gash of North Canyon, heading down to its junction with Marble Canyon in the distance. I did not know it then, but a little venture up North Canyon, some months later, would become the first of those tangent probes that lend enchantment to the crashing froth of a river journey.

On the return my pupil outdistanced me. As I tumbled and wheezed, Dixie cruised right along, hardly slowing for the tricky downhills and curves. The fates, I consoled myself, are responding kindly to her innocence. When I caught up with her, she was buoyant. "Scuba diving's next," she said.

I had planned to camp at the North Rim, 5 miles away by snowmobile to the park boundary, 18 on skis. Visitor snowmobiling is banned in the park. The guides wore long faces; I concurred. There was food and camping gear to haul — a heavy burden — and temperatures dropped to zero at night; in the time allotted, a human anchor on skis was too much.

Somewhat wistfully I watched a guide take off with photographer Tom Bean and Camille Cusumano, a San Francisco writer, as elegant on skis as she was tireless. I had tried to study Camille's technique. Not easy; lithe figures in Lycra do not encourage the study of technique. I circled the baby track near the camp a few times and caught the next van out.

When the snows had gone, I drove back down from Jacob Lake, through the green valley of DeMotte Park and into the national park, the road winding through a forest of fir and spruce and pine and quaking aspen. Some of the aspens wore fringes of green, but many remained a ghostly monochrome tracery. Visitors, thinking green in this season of high spring, often ask, "What happened to the aspens?" And the answer is, give them a week or two. Aspens get their green later than the other trees.

We are above 8,000 feet, and not only the aspens know it. On a day when temperatures at Phantom Ranch ranged between 65° and 90°F, those on the North Rim dipped to 29° and and did not reach 60°. A dawn stroll from Grand Canyon Lodge to Bright Angel Point is a chilly affair, past faded snags and gnarled conifers to the windy tip, and there to shiver as the sun slowly warms the canyon reds and browns as it thaws fingers and toes. Sunrise and sunset—with the twinkle of South Rim lights, the hazy white crowns of the San Francisco Peaks far to the south, and that impossible pink twilight sky—lure strollers to the point. Motorists drive out to sample the fine vistas at Point Imperial and Cape Royal, the Anasazi ruins at Walhalla Glades.

Not many tourists make it to Point Sublime, for the road to Sublime is ridiculous. . . . We made it, 23 miles, gullied and stony. Sego lilies bloomed in the middle of the trail. . . .

Not many tourists make it to Point Sublime, for the road to Sublime is ridiculous. North Rim interpreter Dale Schmidt, who had pedaled out there on his trail bike, thought my sedan just might make it, and his wife, ranger Katy Schmidt, back from a long hike down into the canyon, was willing to join me. We made it, 23 miles, gullied and stony. Sego lilies bloomed in the middle of the trail; penstemon and cliff rose, by the roadside. We spent a fruitless hour or so poking around the edge of a side canyon, looking for the famous Indian granaries located in the ledges and overhangs of Point Sublime.

Strangely, I was not disappointed when we failed to find them. A few years ago it would have been no trouble to find the site, for tourist helicopters rattled into the canyon and hovered before the caves. Environmentalists hung banners to shoo away the choppers. Some, according to the Schmidts, took even more drastic action. "They came down to the caves and stripped and waved at the helicopters," Katy told me. "The copters didn't stay too long." In 1988 new park regulations banned such flights. And now Katy could not even find the caves. The ancient shelters rest in peace.

The promontory of Point Sublime penetrates far into the canyon. The South Rim lies but seven miles away. Eastward, beyond low cliffs, rises vast, flat-topped Shiva Temple—"the grandest of all the buttes and the most majestic in aspect," wrote Clarence Dutton.

I had stayed away from Clarence Dutton as long as I could. The title of his famous work has all the flavor of boiled spinach spiced with sand: *Tertiary*

History of the Grand Cañon District. If any appetite survives, the opening may quickly banish it, with the heading, "Abstract of the Monograph." Ultimately, though, Dutton was unavoidable.

Like John Wesley Powell, Dutton was a Union veteran of the Civil War with a scientific bent. He joined Powell's surveys of the Southwest, and in his monograph—the first one published by the United States Geological Survey—interwove chapters of geology and description. His was the first important geological book on the Grand Canyon. While Dutton's theory of canyon cutting, dubbed the "Great Denudation," no longer stands on the frontiers of science, his literary artistry remains the state of the art in Grand Canyon narrative. It reached its peak right here at Point Sublime:

"The supreme views are to be obtained at the extremities of the long promontories. . . . sitting upon the edge we contemplate the most sublime and awe-inspiring spectacle in the world. . . . In all the vast space beneath and around us there is very little upon which the mind can linger restfully. It is completely filled with objects of gigantic size and amazing form. . . . Hundreds of these mighty structures, miles in length, and thousands of feet in height, rear their majestic heads out of the abyss, displaying their richly-molded plinths and friezes, thrusting out their gables, wing-walls, buttresses, and pilasters, and recessed with alcoves and panels. . . .

"It is completely filled with objects of gigantic size. . . . Hundreds of these mighty structures, miles in length, and thousands of feet in height, rear their majestic heads out of the abyss. . . ."

"At length, as the sun draws near the horizon, the great drama of the day begins. . . . The haze has relaxed its steely glare and has changed to a veil of transparent blue. Slowly the myriads of details have come out and the walls are flecked with lines of minute tracery, forming a diaper of light and shade. . . . The colossal buttes expand in every dimension. Their long, narrow wings, which once were folded together and flattened against each other, open out, disclosing between them vast alcoves illumined with Rembrandt lights tinged with the pale refined blue of the ever-present haze. . . .

"The western sky is all aflame. The scattered banks of cloud and wavy cirrhus have caught the waning splendor, and shine with orange and crimson. Broad slant beams of yellow light, shot through the glory-rifts, fall on turret and tower, on pinnacled crest and winding ledge. . . . The summit band is brilliant yellow; the next below is pale rose. But the grand expanse within is a deep, luminous, resplendent red. The climax has now come. The blaze of sunlight poured over an illimitable surface of glowing red is flung back into the gulf, and, commingling with the blue haze, turns it into a sea of purple of most imperial hue—so rich, so strong, so pure that it makes the heart ache and the throat tighten."

I have seen many a western sky flame over the Grand Canyon—never so gorgeously as now, in the flat light of high noon, with Clarence Dutton's book, at Point Sublime.

The park sweeps westward from Point Sublime, bending with the curves of the Colorado River. There, after threading more gullied roads and hiking for hours along slopes adorned with flowering cactus and cushions of pink and white phlox, some companions and I climbed into a prehistoric rock shelter. Across its sloping back wall, some 7 feet high by 60 feet wide, spread images of birds and humans and other animals that were painted some 2,000 to 4,000 years ago. This is Shamans' Gallery, believed to have been a major ceremonial center for ancient canyon dwellers and considered today a treasure of southwestern prehistoric art. The images, painted in white, red, maroon, green, yellow, and orange, include more than 40 humanlike figures in a variety of forms—small ones with flattened heads, a headless torso, stick figures, bent bodies with outstretched hands, and, most notable, 18 abstract, elongated figures jammed together. The artists were also probably the religious leaders here, suggests archaeologist Polly Schaafsma, who studied the panel. Near the middle of the paintings a boulder has been worn smooth by gallery sitters. Only its remoteness guards Shamans' Gallery from vandals; once more park archaeologist Jan Balsom asked that the route and location be held in confidence.

"A home with ruffled curtains at the windows and flowers blooming on the sills," wrote historian Juanita Brooks, "with a piano and books and magazines, and easy chairs covered with bright chintz is as refreshing to the soul of one wandering in the mazes of The Strip as is the drink of water to the lips." Such a refreshment is the home of Ed, Cathy, Eli, and Kaelin Cummins, 60 miles from pavement, 8 miles from the brink of Toroweap Overlook.

Ed is the park ranger at Tuweep station. Cathy, his wife, is a former ranger. Eli, three years old when I got my hands on him, was king of the hill—expert on dinosaurs, master boulder-scrambler, and Dad's favorite helper. Ten months before my visit Cathy came to term. She and Ed and Eli started out, across 60 miles of dirt road, then another 50 or so of paved highway, to the hospital at St. George, Utah.

"I made Ed stop with every contraction," Cathy recalled. "We had the equipment right in the car, and we could have delivered by the side of the road."

They made it to the hospital. The result was the blue-eyed cherub named Kaelin, now an adventurous crawler with an appetite for juniper berries and gravel. Each night she got a body check for cactus spines.

The Tuweep ranger station was established in 1934. Eli and Kaelin are the first children to live there. Barring unforeseen circumstance, they're set for years; their parents are already collecting home-teaching catalogues. Ed is from San Francisco; Cathy hails from Los Angeles. Increasingly, during their years with the Park Service, they had chosen homes outside of cities. "It was a natural evolution," Cathy told me. "We have no grand philosophical reasoning. We like it here."

Eight miles to the south of their home is the reason for the ranger station — the frightening drop of the Toroweap Overlook at the canyon rim. Ed joined photographer Danny Lehman and me at the campground there. We walked toward the brink.

"People think the river is straight down," Ed told us. "But if you inch close enough to the edge, you can see a substantial ledge, the roof of the Redwall limestone, projecting out. If the river was at the level of the rim here, you would have to walk half a mile to get to it." It took a while before we were prepared to belly down and crawl to the edge to test this hypothesis. It is true. Upright, however, on two legs — as close as most of us get — there is no question about it: The Colorado is straight down, 3,000 feet below, and never mind the Redwall ledge. The Supai sandstone under our feet will do just fine.

There are other interesting views, pleasanter to contemplate from the sandstone boulders of Toroweap: the volcanic mass of Mount Trumbull to the northwest; cinder cones across the river on the Hualapai Reservation; a nearer cone, Vulcans Throne, just to the west, and from it, lava cascading down to the river, million-year-old rock, the youngest in the Grand Canyon. And in the river is Lava Falls, the meanest rapids in the canyon. I stared at it often. With the naked eye I saw a distant white tongue of water, an interlude in the long, green ribbon. Through binoculars I could see it bounding and flailing, yet still remote, unthreatening. It was time to get down there.

Winter magic lures a cross-country skier 18 miles to Bright Angel Point on the North Rim of the canyon. FOLLOWING PAGES: Fall flurries enhance the serenity and majestic seclusion of an aspen grove.

TOM BEAN (OPPOSITE AND FOLLOWING PAGES)

GARY LADD; JACK W. DYKINGA (OPPOSITE)

*Subtle paints from nature's palette glaze
sandstone cliffs of Buckskin Gulch (above),
a side canyon of the Paria. Born from
ancient dunes, the rock shows horizontal
cross-bedding typical of windblown sand,
and mahogany-hued desert varnish. Paria
walls (opposite) shine with similar stain.*

144

DANNY LEHMAN

Mysterious relics of an ancient race, pictographs have adorned Shamans' Gallery
for at least 2,000 years. Art and artifacts endure throughout canyon country.

TOM BEAN; GREG PROBST (OPPOSITE); JACK W. DYKINGA (FOLLOWING PAGES)

*A*utumn's gold brushes aspens
on a forested steep near Cape Royal
(opposite). Maples brighten a slope
of Transept Canyon (above); beyond
rise twin peaks called Brahma and
Zoroaster Temples. Classical mythology
and Eastern religions inspired these
and many other canyon names.

FOLLOWING PAGES: *Near Cape Royal,
stark silhouettes reflect the North Rim's
character: rugged yet reserved, never
revealing all its charms at once.*

149

The River

C rashing waves engulf raft and rafters at Lava Falls,
most violent navigable stretch of the Colorado.
Each year 22,000 people run the river through the canyon.

TOM BEAN; DAVE EDWARDS (PRECEDING PAGES)

*L*ike pilgrims in the hush of a Gothic cathedral, boaters drift deep within the Grand Canyon; along the way side canyons open up like transepts and cloistered gardens.

The boatman tasted the air, inhaling slowly as she leaned into her oars. "Smell the river?" she prodded her passengers. Yes, we nodded, we could smell the cold, moist breath of the Colorado. "I dream about this smell all winter long," Elena Kirschner smiled, settling contentedly into her first Grand Canyon run of the season. The river had a bracing, out-of-season bite. Winter had passed; the depths of the canyon, where the Colorado flowed, baked in desert heat. Yet the Colorado ran cold. It always runs cold. Once upon a time the river ran with the seasons, warm and cold. It ran swiftly in the season of spate, freighting Rocky Mountain runoff to the sea; and after the ebbing of the snowmelt came the season of low water flowing past broad, sandy beaches.

How flows the river today? Forget the season. This is the new Colorado. Dial 1-800-752-8525: "Good morning. This is the Bureau of Reclamation at Glen Canyon Dam. Today is May 15, 1990. Water data for the Colorado River and Lake Powell as of midnight last night follows. . . . The predicted flow pattern from Glen Canyon Dam for today is as follows: Between the hours of midnight and 7 a.m. the flow will be approximately 5,000 cubic feet per second, gradually increasing between 8 a.m. and 6 p.m. to a peak of approximately 17,000 cfs, then decreasing. . . ."

This is the new river of daily "tides"—tides driven not by the moon but by the sun, which brings on hot daylight hours of air-conditioning and peak demand for electrical power. The powers that be have found that the least expensive, most efficient way to satisfy peak demand is to open the dam that controls the river just above Grand Canyon and let Lake Powell spin the turbines. How flows the river today? How hot is it in Phoenix?

From my motel room in Page, the new town beside the dam in northernmost Arizona, I looked out on a distant patch of gray-blue water walled by the undrowned heights of Glen Canyon. It was just a sliver of the nearly 200-mile-long backup that can hold some 9 trillion gallons of the Colorado River.

More than a century ago, John Wesley Powell paid handsome tribute to the "curious ensemble of wonderful features—carved walls, royal arches, glens, alcove gulches, mounds, and monuments. From which of these features shall we

Tranquil pool mirrors sunbathed rock in North Canyon. Many such wild corners along the river tempt visitors to linger and explore. The Grand Canyon, wrote Major Powell, is "a composite of thousands, of tens of thousands, of gorges."

TOM TILL

select a name? We decided to call it Glen Canyon." Lake Powell, which inundated so many of these wonderful features, is not without wonders. There are surely pleasures on the lake, and beauty in the rock that remains above it. For all that drowned, Powell's words and latter-day albums of nostalgia will have to do.

I had come not to wallow in the lake, but to ride the Colorado flowing through the Grand Canyon it had cut, walloping into the boulder gardens strewn across its path. I joined a river trip sponsored by the Grand Canyon Trust, devoted to protecting not only the canyon but also the resources of the entire physiographic province of which the canyon is a part—the 130,000-square-mile Colorado Plateau spreading north-, south-, and eastward. We launched 16 miles below the dam at Lees Ferry, the head of the Grand Canyon and the only spot where rim and river are just about level with each other. The Kaibab limestone, the rimrock that sits a mile or more above the Colorado on the park's North Rim, here lies below ground. On the bustling shore there is little to recall the days of the ferry, or the dark history of the first ferryman, John Doyle Lee.

*T*he Kaibab limestone . . . here lies below
    ground. On the bustling shore there is little
to recall the days of the ferry, or the dark history
    of the first ferryman, John Doyle Lee.

He was an adopted son of Brigham Young and a central figure in the Mountain Meadows Massacre of 1857. There in southwestern Utah, amid bitter hatreds and looming war with federal troops, Mormons and Indians slaughtered more than a hundred California-bound emigrants. In 1872 Lee, a hunted man, excommunicated by his church, moved here to the banks of the Colorado. A few months later he and "Mrs. Lee XVIII" (as chronicler Frederick Dellenbaugh called her) hosted the second Powell expedition. Three crewmen having departed, Powell abandoned one of his boats. It became Lee's first ferry. Lee was captured, convicted, and in 1877 brought to the scene of the massacre for execution. He sat on his coffin and faced a firing squad with a plea that surely deserves mention in the anthologies of famous last words: "Center my heart, boys. Don't mangle my body!" He was the only one of the killers brought to justice, a scapegoat, or as the diligent Mormon historian Juanita Brooks termed it, "An Official Sacrifice."

The Colorado begins with glacial trickles in the Colorado Rockies and nearly 14,000 feet above sea level in the Wind River Range of Wyoming. At Lees Ferry it has descended to 3,116 feet. In the first 237 miles of the 277-mile-long Grand Canyon it drops almost 2,000 feet, averaging 8 feet to the mile. For much of the distance, however, the Colorado slopes gently; some hundred rapids, totaling less than a tenth of the river's length in the canyon, account for more than half the drop. Amid the armadas of inflated neoprene—small rafts and big "baloney boats" with motors—the dories of the Grand Canyon, gaily painted in blues and whites and reds, exude an air of breeding, of vintage. Their very name suggests it. They descend from the McKenzie River fishing dories of Oregon, with decking and watertight compartments added so that they can take a swamping and stay afloat. Their power is vintage power: river current, augmented by strong arms cranking 10- or 11-foot oars. They do not offer the fastest or the cheapest ride, but seem well suited for savoring the adventurous traditions of river running—though John Wesley Powell with his waterlogged stores and battered vessels could only dream of the epicurean amenities the dory trips offer.

A dozen of us settled fore and aft in five boats, some of wood, some of metal; the company included a crew of nine and Martin Litton, who had resisted the trend toward inflatables and helped bring the dories to the Colorado in the early 1960s. A few miles downstream from our launch, bobbing gently, we passed under the silver tracery of the Navajo Bridge, which had replaced John Doyle Lee's ferry. We were in no hurry; early in the day the river was on night water, too low for the dories in some serious rapids just ahead. Though the turbines at the dam produce electricity rapidly, the releases run downstream at an average speed of four miles an hour. So we lolled away the morning. As we floated, the canyon walls rose quickly, layer upon familiar layer—Kaibab limestone, Toroweap, Coconino, Hermit shale; and when boatman Pete Gross rested his oars and broke out his recorder, the rising walls channeled the strains of "Greensleeves," a bit of Mendelssohn, and the "Ode to Joy" from Beethoven's Ninth Symphony.

An early lunch stop gave the river more time to rise; we watched it come up on an unfailing river gauge, a stick stuck in the sand at river's edge. Here trip leader Kenton Grua and the boatmen showed us how to help them keep a boat from flipping—by high-siding, leaning into the breaking waves, never the other way, which helps the waves. Capsizing in the dories is neither rare nor common; it happens, and with it, sometimes bumps and bruises.

Unique in so many ways, the canyon has its own 10-point rating system for the rapids. Generally, said boatman Jeff Schloss, canyon ratings are about twice what they would be on the national 6-point scale. In contrast to small whitewater streams that require constant maneuvering, Jeff said, "the Colorado is a big, pushy river, with the entrances to the rapids very important, and there's not much maneuvering once you get in."

Like most rapids in the canyon, Badger Creek, at mile 8, gets easier with higher water. According to Larry Stevens's popular river guide, Badger rates an 8 at very low water, dropping to a 5 in high water. As we approached, birdsong along the cliffs gradually gave way to the low rumble of the rapids, formed by debris fans spewed from Badger Creek on the right and Jackass Creek on the left. The hazard at Badger, said Jeff, is setting up too far to the right and smacking down hard into a rock-studded hole of churning white water. At high water, Jeff went on, "you can run the hole and hope to have enough momentum to punch through to the other side. But if you don't punch through, you can turn sideways, and the water pouring down into the hole turns you over. At this low water level, though, we'd hit the rock, so we'll miss the hole and take the waves in the middle." Which we did, dead center down a tongue into the first of the great wave trains of the Grand Canyon rapids, edging by the treacherous hole, bumping merrily along, cutting into, over, and down the waves.

A few miles farther, Soap Creek Rapids seemed even more of a seesaw, greeting us with a ten-foot wave, angling the boat up so that in the bow I saw nothing but sky, following with a slam dunk deep into a trough that lathered us with a foaming breaker. Someone thought Soak Creek would be a better name. The dousing chilled us. Released from the depths of Lake Powell, the water starts down at around 48°F, warming up about a degree a day as it courses the canyon.

Around Sheer Wall Rapids three bighorn sheep posed on a shelf above us—littlehorns actually, ewes, perhaps a lamb, blending nicely with the red Supai rock.

Around Sheer Wall Rapids three bighorn sheep posed on a shelf above us—littlehorns actually, ewes, perhaps a lamb, blending nicely with the red Supai rock. House Rock Rapids, less of a drop than Soap or Badger, rates tougher; a debris fan from Rider Canyon dams half the Colorado, funneling the river into a narrow tongue with lots of white licks that bottoms out in a giant hole. Strategy here calls for powelling, rowing backward, the standard position for Powell's boatmen.

"It's almost as if there's a fence on the water that you have to break through to get into the slow water on the right," said Jeff. "If you push into it gently, you won't break through, and it'll just slide you right into the hole. You can go much faster by powelling." We ended up punching through backward. We entered the funnel at the right of center, turned broadside in the thick of the waves. Jeff powelled hard across the "fence," and the bow spun downstream.

A mile or so ahead we looked up at a nondescript little memorial to the Colorado of once upon a time. Out of the river rose a boulder some 20 feet high. On it lay a jumble of tree trunks, a reminder of the "unregulated" river, whose flow, in years of record runoff, might reach 200,000 cubic feet per second. The turbines at the dam, in contrast, have a peak discharge of 33,200 cfs; in 1983, a year of high runoff, the dam's spillways were opened. The river barreled through at 92,600 cfs, but never reached the top of the boulder; the driftwood remained, a memento of the wild Colorado of old.

"The Grand Canyon of the Colorado," Powell reported, "is a canyon composed of many canyons. It is a composite of thousands, of tens of thousands, of gorges." We stopped for the night, set out the bedding, and followed the boatmen into the magic of North Canyon, away from the rumble of the rapids that North Canyon debris had formed. The day's rocking and pounding were behind us. The intimacy and serenity of the side canyon—the first of many—took over, the effect as surprising and memorable as the crashing waves.

A thread of water sluiced down North Canyon and billowed into a pool, beside which a lone willow grew. A high-pitched chorus of canyon tree frogs surrounded us. Red walls of sandstone curved away like a goblet as they rose, fracturing and spalling off in vertical planes. Kenton Grua, in the first of his rock talks, discussed the phenomenon. Jeff Schloss, distance runner and skiing racer, traversed the smooth concavity of 280-million-year-old rock. Pete Gross brought out a guitar and sang a Joni Mitchell song; its refrain, heard again and again as our days ebbed into evening, became for me a leitmotiv of the trip:

> And the seasons, they go round and round,
> And the painted ponies go up and down.
> We're captives on the carousel of time.
> We can't return,
> We can only look behind from where we came. . . .

So there was more to the river trip than splash and dash, and, clearly, more to the crew as well. Three men and two women rowed dories. Martin Litton frequently took a turn at the oars. There were two other oarsmen, women who had confronted white water in the Rockies and who hoped in time to row Grand Canyon dories. For this trip they rowed the heavy-laden supply rafts. In addition, Jan Kempster turned the trip into a movable feast; folks who had known the good life from San Francisco to Martha's Vineyard raved about her cookery. Alison French Steen sang folk songs, cursed at the daily pile of unwieldy duffles she had to lash to her raft, hiked the side canyons at every opportunity, and squeezed through the narrowest and slipperiest of rock niches.

Next morning I rode with Elena Kirschner, still intoxicated with the fresh river smell, her winter's dream come true. No lolling today; the river was dropping, and we had to run the Roaring Twenties—the feisty rapids 20 to 30 miles out from mile zero—before the low flow turned feisty rapids into threatening ones. Yet we did not leave until the campsite was picked clean of any sign of our presence. Camping spots are limited and precious; 22,000 river runners use them every year. From personal conviction and commercial self-interest, the boatmen work hard to keep from fouling them. And the Park Service sees to it.

At 24-Mile Rapids, a tame little run until debris from a flash flood had earned it an 8 rating at very low water, the problem was hole right and hole left. The solution was the slot between them. Elena threaded it neatly; not everyone did, though all stayed right side up.

"It would be most embarrassing," said Elena after Cave Springs Rapids around mile 26, "if we flipped today from here on in. If you're gonna flip, it would be best to do it in an honorable spot, and the honorable spots for this day are behind us." And it was here, in a kittenish stretch of the Colorado, that I discovered the joys of bowriding—straddling the bow, with legs hanging over the sides. Bowriding makes kittenish waves interesting, and the occasional interesting wave punishing. The wave does not break over the bow; it breaks over the squat figurehead, who shivers and sheds water and screams, "Hey, this is great!"

> "We have cut through the sandstones
> and limestones met in the upper part
> of the canyon, and through one great bed
> of marble a thousand feet in thickness."

By then the rising canyon walls had revealed the soaring cliffs responsible for the enduring misnomer attached to the first 60 miles of the canyon. "At last the storm ceases," Powell wrote, "and we go on. We have cut through the sandstones and limestones met in the upper part of the canyon, and through one great bed of marble a thousand feet in thickness. In this, great numbers of caves are hollowed out, and carvings are seen which suggest architectural forms. . . . As this great bed forms a distinctive feature of the canyon, we call it Marble Canyon." That bed is not marble; it is the gray, red-stained wall that we call Redwall limestone. Historian C. Gregory Crampton suggests that Powell used marble "in its structural and architectural sense."

The Redwall gleamed in the sunlight and mirrored itself in the river as we glided through soft ripples. Swallows twittered, and canyon wrens sang. We stopped to poke around in South Canyon, rich in history and prehistory and mystery. Here 4,000-year-old split-twig figurines were discovered in a cave, and a skeleton with broken legs was found. We floated slowly by Vasey's Paradise, named for a botanist. Here water gushes out of the Redwall and nurtures a luxuriant growth: watercress, poison ivy, columbine, monkeyflower. We tied up a mile beyond it to wander about immense Redwall Cavern. Pete unsheathed his recorder; the acoustics of the high, domed chamber gave him fine support.

We hiked up Nautiloid Canyon to see the fossils it was named for. They lie embedded in the rock pavement, squidlike cephalopods that looked like chambered nautiluses, but uncoiled and stretched flat. Around mile 39 we saw the spoil heaps and test borings of the proposed Marble Canyon dam. "If they had built it," observed Elena, "we would have been traveling on a lake from Lees Ferry to here." Instead, a nationwide protest stirred by the Sierra Club drowned the proposal, and also defeated plans for the Bridge Canyon Dam downstream.

Buck Farm Canyon seemed ideal for camping—fine sandy beach, a grove of tamarisks for privacy, a skyful of bats that darted to and fro across our flashlight beams. The sand was fine all right; indeed, like sugar. When the breeze stirred, it sent grains against our bedrolls, our faces, our teeth. In all, a gritty night. Next morning, Kenton glanced up at Martin Litton. "Did you do your wind dance?" No. Martin had forgotten the ritual dance that calms the headwinds on the river and keeps the sand down in camp. "Before the dam," Martin grumbled, "we were able to camp on damp beaches, and there was no sand blowing. Now we're lucky to find sand to camp on."

Before the dam, the season of high runoff scoured the beaches, but as the river subsided, it replenished them with some of the 50 to 500 million tons of sediment it carried through the canyon each year. Now most of the silt sinks to the bottom of Lake Powell. Runoff from major side canyons still brings in some silt, but the beaches have shrunk and, without corrective action, may vanish.

Whatever the beaches looked like at Nankoweap Creek before the dam, they remain spacious and inviting today, favored by backpackers and river travelers. Here the tight confines of Marble Canyon begin to widen out toward the sprawl of buttes and mesas familiar to visitors on the park rims. Prehistoric people favored Nankoweap as well; more than 40 sites have been found. During the evening we camped here, streams of hikers wheezed several hundred feet up the talus slopes to peer into hollow rock chambers that once were granaries—and to sit by them and look south at the river gliding and the canyon vista widening.

I scanned the high rim just across the river, the Marble Platform—Navajo land—searching for the spot where I had spent an evening and a morning with Dave Wegner peering through a spotting scope. For most of a decade Dave has managed a multimillion-dollar program of environmental studies to determine the impact of the dam and to work out some remedies. In Washington, D.C.,

I have heard Dave referred to as *the* environmentalist in the Bureau of Reclamation. He calls himself an endangered species, targeted by engineers, developers, and the traditions of his agency, and by recreationists who see data pile up without action. When we camped up there on the Blue Moon Bench of the Marble Platform, it was Dave's first day off in six months. He did not surprise me when he focused on his team of observers encamped at Nankoweap and cried out, half-seriously: "C'mon you guys! There's eagles out there, and those guys are sitting around eating breakfast." Thirty-five hundred feet below us, the team heard nothing. But they knew all about the eagles.

Before the dam, bald eagles were probably rare in the Grand Canyon. Then, as cold, clear water flowed through the canyon from the depths of Lake Powell, trout, an exotic here, flourished, while native warm-water fishes suffered severely. For a time the waters just below the dam, stocked with rainbows by the state, won national renown as a "premier trophy fishery."

The trout spread downstream. Now, in winter and early spring, trout turn up Nankoweap Creek to spawn. And as we watched, bald eagles, huge wings outspread, crisscrossed over the creek. Frequently one would flutter to the water, pause for a moment, then fly off a short distance, land, and start bending its beak to its talons. Fishing and feasting.

One wants to lock in those hours—sitting on the limestone rim, feet hanging over with nothing but air for thousands of feet below, the Grand Canyon cliffs pink and tan and red, the shaley slopes grizzled with snow, an east wind snapping, looking down on eagles.

Bryan Brown, a consulting ornithologist, was camped down there. He has been watching the eagles for some years. "It's the largest concentration of wintering and migrating bald eagles in the entire Southwest," he told me in a later interview. "Seventy to a hundred may have moved through in February and March, the peak time of spawning. Ravens would surround the eagles. One would pull at an eagle's tail, and another would run around front and steal a piece of fish. Golden eagles were fishing too, but the ravens wouldn't go near them. No one messes around with golden eagles."

(*Continued on page 177*)

Last minute details busy boaters at Lees Ferry, starting point for river trips through the canyon. FOLLOWING PAGES: Boatmen ready a raft to run Badger Creek, the first major rapids encountered on the river.

TOM BEAN; JOSEF MUENCH (FOLLOWING PAGES)

*F*orbidding spikes of an agave (opposite)
belie its role as a food of ancient canyon
peoples. The agave, or century plant,
sends up a flower stalk after 10 to 30 years,
then dies. Vivid blooms of beavertail cactus
brighten arid corners. Fleshy stems and
waxy coating retain moisture and adapt
such plants to harsh desert conditions.

©LARRY ULRICH; TOM TILL (OPPOSITE)

TOM BEAN

*T*races of the ancients touch modern-day visitors to the canyon. High above the river at Nankoweap, hikers pause on a ledge outside small chambers built into the base of the Redwall a thousand years ago. Anasazi Indians stored grain here to protect it from rodents and weather. These "ancient ones" inhabited thousands of sites in the Grand Canyon, then moved on, leaving only hints of their occupation. Rock art, such as a handprint (below) on a sandstone face at Deer Creek Narrows, offers a glimpse of prehistoric culture in the canyon.

DAVE EDWARDS

TOM BEAN

*H*igh and dry at Hance Rapids, boaters endure forced leisure, hoping for a hot day in Phoenix; low demand for electricity can mean low water — and stranded dories.

I asked Bryan about the overall impact of the dam. "It almost sounds like heresy for me to say this," he replied. "The dam has done horrible things to the environment. But it's an undeniable fact that the dam has had some positive effects." With an upsurge in insect life and a spread of vegetation through what used to be the scour zone, the numbers of birds breeding along the river increased five- or tenfold. The increase of swifts and swallows—and bats as well—seems to have benefited an endangered predator; a 1989 survey discovered 58 pairs of peregrine falcons within the park, perhaps the largest known population in the lower 48.

In a new book, Bryan Brown and Steven W. Carothers assert that the river "is no longer natural, but instead is *naturalized,* a blend of the old and the new, a mixture of native and the exotic organisms." A new vision is needed, the authors say, for there is currently "no guidance for coping with naturalized ecosystems."

When the dories floated by Nankoweap Creek, the spawning was over, the eagles were gone. Night and the dark cliffs enfolded all but a patch of starlit sky, and the folksingers reminded us once more that we were "captives on the carousel of time."

As the boatmen scouted and threaded and bucked the rapids, I thought more and more that this is their show—theirs the knowledge, the strength, the adrenaline pumping. Occasionally some of us tried the oars, but only in quieter water. There was also an inflatable two-person kayak, not much more than a toy, really. Jim Carrier, a Denver columnist, and I decided to run it through Kwagunt Rapids, no more than a respectable 6 on the canyon scale, but the most respectable of any we faced on the day after Nankoweap. Kwagunt—named for a Paiute who lived in the area—swamped us, hammered us, spun us around, and spit us out in good shape, to the cheers of the nearby boats. What went right? As usual, I relied on Fishbein's first law of buoyancy: A boat likes to float; when in doubt, do nothing; let it float. Jim, I suspect, wielded a more sophisticated paddle in the stern, for Kwagunt has a mean hole that properly rewards the sin of sloth.

The run renewed my curiosity about how an open canoe, my preferred craft, would do on the Colorado. In the summer of 1990 Ed Grove, a neighbor

W*rinkles of time: A geologist describes fractures in the walls of 75-Mile Canyon. Shinumo quartzite, a silica-cemented sandstone a billion years old, forms this rock face. River runners read an ever-varied geologic chronicle.*

TOM BEAN

and fellow member of the Canoe Cruisers Association of Washington, ran the river in an open canoe, rigged so that it could be rolled after a flip. "In the East," he told me, "you have to maneuver much more to avoid rocks, drowned trees, and holes. The Colorado is generally straightforward. The rapids are very similar, with huge wave trains. If you turn over and have a good life jacket and hang on to your boat, there is not much to hit on the bottom." Ed also noted with pride that "you don't have to be a young, aggressive expert open-boater to do the canyon. Our group of grizzled grayhairs had an average age of 45, and most of us were advanced rather than expert boaters."

N either storm nor runoff had muddied the waters of the Little Colorado when we beached at its mouth, and Kenton summoned us to revels in the warm, blue stream.

Neither storm nor runoff had muddied the waters of the Little Colorado when we beached at its mouth, and Kenton summoned us to revels in the warm, blue stream. He led us along 550-million-year-old sandstone ledges, then showed us how to step into our life jackets and fasten them so that they looked like huge, unsinkable diapers. And then we plunged into the Little Colorado and chuted feet first, singly or in chains of eight or more, down a shallow flume, bumping back and forth between white boulders.

Out of my vast trove of clichés, I had called up "reserved British barrister" to describe my frequent boatmate Graham Child. At the Little Colorado the tired image collapsed. The vacationing London lawyer waddled along in his orange diaper, as silly looking as the rest of us, and when he floated down the rocky slope, his fair, freckled face beamed like a sunflower against the blue water.

There's much more serious business around the mouth of the Little Colorado. Here Dave Wegner's researchers are making exhaustive studies of the most critical remaining habitat in the canyon for the native and endangered humpback chub, one of the relics of the old, warm Colorado. Other warm-water natives—the Colorado squawfish, the bonytail chub, and the razorback sucker—could not cope with "naturalization." They are either extirpated in the canyon or very nearly so.

There were no revels for John Wesley Powell. He found the Little Colorado "exceedingly muddy." Here the Major and his crew prepared for the "Great Unknown," resifting flour, salvaging spoiled bacon, redrying waterlogged dried apples. Mention of the Great Unknown would identify this voyage as Powell's pioneering exploration, in 1869. Elsewhere in his classic narrative the Major mingles details of his second run, in 1871-72, without distinguishing.

For us, no Great Unknown lies ahead. Each boatman must make at least six trips before taking on commercial passengers. And Kenton, our leader, is part of the modern legendry of river running here. In the flood year of 1983, with the river running at 72,000 cubic feet per second, Kenton and two companions— Rudi Petschek and Steve Reynolds—took off on a speed run. They ran day and night, and pulled out at Grand Wash Cliffs in 36 hours, 38 minutes, and 29 seconds—lopping more than 10 hours off the previous record for oared boats. Kenton didn't tell me this: I read it in a book. Nor did he tell me of his trip to Washington some years ago with his wife, Denice Napoletano, another of our boatmen. Ed Norton of the Grand Canyon Trust briefed Kenton in advance on the places to see in the nation's capital. They met for lunch on the first day. "Did you see any of them?" Ed asked. "No," Kenton replied, "I thought it would be nice to go down to Arlington National Cemetery and put some flowers on the grave of the Major and Emma." Emma was Mrs. Powell.

We passed by the old Hopi salt mines in the Tapeats sandstone, and before long were in sight of Desert View and Lipan Point, popular viewpoints on the park's South Rim. The boatmen fought headwinds for hours, maneuvering to gain what help they could find in the downstream segments of eddy swirls. The headwinds slowed us. At Unkar Creek, low water tripped us up. A gravel bar extended pretty much across the river, forcing us to squiggle between rocks. My boat, one of the wooden ones, missed a squiggle, took a light hit that stove a few inches of chine, and began to ship water.

We found a beach, ran the boat up on an inflated roller tube—the answer to the backbreaking portage of olden days—and Kenton broke out the repair kit. I recalled what one of the boatmen had told me a few days before: "The dories are beautiful and responsive and great fun, but they are unforgiving." At just the right moment, as we fidgeted in the glaring heat, Jeff Schloss siphoned us off for a hike up 75-Mile Canyon. There, in blessed shade, we walked with the smooth, flowing curves of Shinumo quartzite walls, water-cut and water-polished purple rock splashed with streaks of tan. Another side canyon, another surprise, another delight.

If Unkar tripped us up, Hance Rapids, four miles downstream, stopped us cold. Hance, long and tricky, rates the ultimate 10 at very low water, and the water was very low. Hance was a fury of rock and blasting waves, white water wall-to-wall for hundreds of yards. The boatmen scouted one side and then the other. "We checked every channel we could find," said Jeff. "There was a rock at the bottom of every single one." Said Kenton: "Hance is unrunnable for dories."

The problem was weekend water. Demand for peak power, and, therefore, the river flow, drop on weekends. This was Sunday. Monday brought no relief. Phoenix might be at work in cool comfort, but the water that turned the turbines at Glen Canyon Dam would take a day to reach us here.

So for a long, desultory day we became shade-worshiping lotus eaters becalmed beside bright red cliffs of Hakatai shale, composing foul imprecations upon the infernal fluctuating flows. Are the fluctuations necessary? The main purpose of Glen Canyon Dam is to let the states of the upper Colorado basin—Utah, Colorado, Wyoming, and New Mexico—store their share of river water while assuring the allotted deliveries to downstream states and Mexico. Storage and apportionment of the water do not require hydropower generation. But the law provided for the turbines as a "cash register" to help pay for the dam and irrigation projects; the register rings up some 80 million dollars a year.

The Western Area Power Administration, an agency of the U.S. Department of Energy, which markets the hydropower, insists that its mandate is to run the power plant at the "most productive rate." That view has repeatedly been challenged by environmentalists and river users. Research on the post-dam river has been going on for years. In 1989 the Secretary of the Interior ordered an Environmental Impact Statement that will evaluate the possible alternatives to the current operation of the dam and their impacts on downstream environmental and recreational resources. Perhaps most important, the EIS process requires a decision and public involvement.

Despite the heat at Hance, the side canyons lured a number of us. Some chose a serious reach up Red Canyon on the Hance Trail. Pete Gross, Denice Napoletano, Alison Steen, and I rowed a mile upstream to Papago Canyon. There we slithered up narrow chutes to a shaded ledge frequented by an assortment of lizards and a black-chinned hummingbird; and on the cool rock, in the fragrance of desert bloom—honey mesquite, Denice thought—we slept.

Tuesday. Good news on the little stick planted in the sand. It was wet; the river was rising. Soon came a thundering herd of baloney boats that had been waiting for water upstream; they caterpillared through Hance and were gone. They can handle lower water in the rapids than the dories can; their biggest problem, I learned, is on the beaches. Should they get stranded, there is no pushing them off. Our jaunty little fleet followed. The two metal dories went first. I rode with Jeff in a wooden dory, just behind them. He thought they had the entrance perfect, but as they slid over into the first chute, we heard a clunk, and then another. Both had scraped rock. Jeff stood up, peering, puzzled: "I don't know what to do." But he did. He lined up a bit to the right, and we went over the ledge without a sound—and then a rush of sound as the bow dug down, snapped up, and waves burst against us from both sides. We floated a brief green respite, steered left around a downstream rock fence, then took the big chute that had had everyone worried. Now higher water cushioned the boulder at the bottom, and all bounced safely out.

We entered Granite Gorge as the canyon bedrock—Vishnu schist and Zoroaster granite—emerged. Schist and the river made for high art; we floated by water-carved rock, gleaming black fluted walls, honeycombs, sharp blades, and weird, elongated forms that reminded me of Giacometti's stringy sculptures.

At Phantom Ranch some of our group departed; others, all interested in the goals of the Grand Canyon Trust, came aboard. Within an hour of pushing off, they were initiated into some of the best running on the river. We avoided the horns—two boulders—of Horn Creek Rapids, crossed its tongue, and catapulted down the wave train. Granite Rapids was like mogul skiing: topping a wave, turning and sliding, and on to the next bump—and beware of the laterals on the right, the waves curling back from the canyon wall. Hermit was a long, straight rockabye shot.

Granite Rapids was like mogul skiing: topping a wave, turning and sliding, and on to the next bump. . . . Hermit was a long, straight rockabye shot.

Next morning came Crystal, little regarded until 1966, when a historic flash flood spewed boulders and other debris out across the river. Without the power of seasonal runoff, the new Colorado has not done much to nudge the debris fan downstream. Crystal rates a solid 10, 10 plus in high water. Some geologists see it as an omen; rapids will continue to build and could eventually become unrunnable. The boatmen scouted Crystal long and carefully; all found the safe green slot Kenton recommended, powelled crisply away from the most fearsome hole, and clumped together in the quiet swirls of "Thank God Eddy" with hoots of relief and triumph.

A day later, as I rode with Denice, a lateral wave at Specter Rapids swung us around and rode us into the canyon wall, cracking the gunwale and a rib just aft of the beam. No great damage. Except that Bedrock was next, a tricky rapid split by a bedrock island, also known as Dreadrock. The mood seemed strained, the scouting unusually long. I think Jim Trees helped get us back on track. Jim, chairman of the Grand Canyon Trust, retired from Wall Street and now a rancher in Utah, had known the boatmen for some years. Now he recalled that he and

Denice once joked about running Bedrock, and he asked if he and his friend Gila Ludwig could join us. So down Bedrock we went, nicely between the island and a spray of boulders. Then Bedrock's tailwaves washed the boat into a strong eddy that waltzed us round and round and wouldn't let go. On the edge of the swirl lay a huge rock, just under the surface; methought I saw that rock blush at what Denice called it as she stroked with all she had to steer clear. On the third go-round we broke out. Denice dropped an oar, turned to me in the stern, and smiled, "Gimme five." I gave her ten.

*D*eer Creek draws a crowd: to the red rock
    alcove where mist clouds a hundred-foot
waterfall; to the slithery slit above . . . to the verdant
copse under a hole in the Muav limestone. . . .

Deer Creek draws a crowd: to the red rock alcove where mist clouds a hundred-foot waterfall; to the slithery slit above, which channels the creek; to the desert garden still higher; to the verdant copse under a hole in the Muav limestone; there to shiver in the shade while Deer Creek washes away the sweat of the hike. A trail leads on to the spectacular fall of Thunder River, some five miles distant.

On the flat, from Powell's day to this, the hazard of the Colorado is boredom. To counter it the Major would read aloud from classics such as Sir Walter Scott's *Marmion* and *Lady of the Lake:* "Harp of the North! that mouldering long hast hung / On the witch-elm that shades Saint Fillan's spring, / And down the fitful breeze thy numbers flung, / Till envious ivy did around thee cling. . . ." Whew! Let's have some rapids.

The corky little kayak helped banish boredom. Jim Trees and I took a turn in it, and in some piddling riffle—not an honorable spot by a long shot—we won the dishonor of producing the only flip on this voyage. We climbed back aboard unharmed, and thereupon ensued a saccharine exchange: "My fault, I turned us over." "No, Jim, I dug in on the low side and flipped it." And on and on. I think I won that argument; none of the boatmen suggested I had missed my calling.

We hiked up into Matkat—Matkatamiba Canyon—wading its creek to a serene, restful amphitheater. I hiked on alone, up the narrowing canyon, unaware of time or distance, until shouts echoing along the walls called me down. One guidebook I read back at the river identified that ground as sacred to the Havasupai. Soon after, Jim, Gila, Graham Child, and I embarked with Elena down Upset Rapids. Confronted simultaneously with a giant wave in front and one from the right, Elena was forced to choose; she plowed directly ahead. The right wave lifted and tilted us steeply to the left, sliding Elena toward the gunwales, one oar dangling, her legs in the air. From the stern Jim pulled her back. Without missing a beat, Elena backed us away from the looming canyon wall, screaming "Bail! Bail!" to get us to lighten the swamped dory. Moral of the story: Do not trespass upon sacred precincts.

Some of our group departed early. We saw them off at Havasu Creek, the blue-green stream that steps down in splendid waterfalls from the roadless canyon home of the Havasupai, the "People of the Blue-green Water." Jeff Schloss, Graham, and I took off to see Mooney, the tallest and most spectacular of the falls, a white flood crashing nearly 200 feet into a blue-green pond rimmed by an amphitheater draped with greenery and brown travertine. We hiked nearly 11 miles round trip back and forth across the creek, over travertine cliffs, on paths choked with grasses and grapevines, amid haunting, unfamiliar birdsong.

Next morning, in the campground sands of National Canyon, Jeff sketched out the challenge of the day: celebrated Lava Falls, most exciting rapids in the canyon. "The middle of the river is a giant ledge," said Jeff, "a guaranteed flip. Our favorite run is to the left of that, left water, which we can do at anywhere from 18,000 to 50,000 cubic feet per second. You won't see that today.

"More likely we'll see slot water or right water. Just to the right of the ledge there is a slot, about the width of a boat, with another hole to the right of that. It's very scary, because the hole below the main ledge is the nastiest place you would ever want to be. If you do everything right, it's almost like a magical highway, a little hidden door that opens up, and you just shoot right through. But an error of just a few inches and you can get into big trouble. I saw Pete flip in the slot a couple of years ago. It's turned a lot of boats over.

"So that's medium flow. Most likely, what we'll have today is right water. This is a series of gigantic, irregular V-shaped waves. You try to get into the apex of each one, it knocks you around, and then you have to straighten out for the next one. If you miss a little bit to one side or the other, you are going sideways into a wave. And they are very explosive, breaking back on the top, anywhere from 6 to 15 feet high.

"We wouldn't mind the right run so much if that was all there was to it. But down at the bottom is a giant chunk of black lava sitting in the river. Just made to eat boats up, right on the edge of the wave train. Sometimes you can reach out and touch that rock as you go by."

Left water, slot water, right water. How about none of the above? "This is crazy water," Kenton scowled, as we stood above the wild reach at Lava Falls, "low for the slot, high for the right." Left, of course, was a minefield of rocks. The holes in the middle and the V-waves on the right looked as if someone had set off depth charges under them.

"Piece of cake?" someone smiled at Kenton. "Yeah," he responded, "upside-down cake."

He invited Graham and me to join him in the first boat through. We angled over an emerald swell and across a lateral wave curling out of a hole, and then straightened into the V-train. Torrents kicked us to and fro. Walls of water raked over us. Trying to help, high-siding into each surge, swamped by it, I had no idea how close to course we held. On the fifth wave—a 15-footer, Kenton thought—the boat spun around like a cork, dug for the bottom, and wallowed within a yard of that gruesome black boulder. In less than a minute it was over. Watching the others was scarier than going through, as we saw boats pounded, flung high, spun about, driven toward the rock—and, just in time, washed around it. All were in harm's way, and no one harmed. After a merry night, we headed for the helicopter landing on Hualapai land at mile 188—and out.

Lava Falls and the side canyons choked with "frozen lava" in this reach remind us that dams are not forever in the Grand Canyon. In the past 1.2 million years more than 150 lava flows have dammed the river at least a dozen times. One dam created a lake that spanned all the distance we had come and far up into present-day Utah, some 324 miles. The river destroyed all of the dams.

"The only way to keep your sanity about Glen Canyon Dam is to think in geologic terms," my rim-to-rim hiking companion, Bill Breed, once told me. "Someday Glen Canyon Dam will silt up and the dam will break down, and the mud and the silt will come through, and it will be the old river again."

I would like to see that, the mighty stream, unfettered, flowing to the majesty of seasonal rhythms. A naive wish, considering the infernal pokiness of geologic time. Still, I had seen enough—in the riot of rock colors, on the hot, sinuous trails, beside shaded pools in hidden crannies, and through the gauntlet of bursting waves—to quiet the doubt raised one snowy winter morning on the South Rim. From rim to river, in any season, canyon country is worth leaving home for.

*L*acework wings spread wide,
a dragonfly rests on a twig;
the insect feeds mostly on mosquitoes.
Insects—as predators and as prey—
form a vital strand in the food web
of the Colorado River corridor.

COBY JORDAN

*S*leek-lined dory Tuolumne *slices through waves at Granite Rapids during the author's trip. Before running the rock-strewn expanse (above), boatman and passengers scout the river. In the 277-mile stretch through the Grand Canyon, the Colorado drops 2,000 feet and thunders over some 70 major rapids.*

FOLLOWING PAGES: Evening rewards long river hours with tranquillity— and a light show, as the setting sun ignites the canyon walls.

TOM BEAN (ABOVE, TOP, AND FOLLOWING PAGES)

RUDI PETSCHEK

*E*phemeral flower, the Colorado four-o'clock blooms for only one day — in striking
contrast to the timeless layers of stone and rock that form the Grand Canyon.

©PAT O'HARA (BOTH); ©LARRY ULRICH (FOLLOWING PAGES)

*C*olors of paradise tint terraced pools
of Havasu Creek. The stream takes its hue
from calcium carbonate in the waters that
calcifies into travertine terraces. Near
Havasu Falls (above), a flash flood in the
summer of 1990 scoured the travertine.

FOLLOWING PAGES: Sunrise gleams on
calm waters near Kanab Creek. The
"Colorado is the soul of the desert,"
wrote Edward Abbey, lyrical voice of the
Southwest. "Brave boatmen come, they
go, they die, the river flows on forever."

ACKNOWLEDGMENTS

The Book Division is grateful to the individuals, groups, and organizations named or quoted in the text and to those cited here for their assistance during the production of this Special Publication: Chuck Lundy, Jerry Mitchell, John C. O'Brien, and Greer Price of Grand Canyon National Park.

We also thank the following people for so generously sharing their experience and expertise with us: George H. Billingsley, Tom Britt, Michael Collier, Tom Folks, Greg Foote, Scott Madsen, Eckhart Melotki, Molly Ross, and Dave Sabo.

We wish to thank the following copyright holder for permission to reprint material on page 161 of the text:

"THE CIRCLE GAME"
(Joni Mitchell)
©1966, 1974, SIQUOMB PUBLISHING CORP.
All Rights Reserved. Used by Permission.

Composition for this book by the Typographic section of National Geographic Producton Services, Pre-Press Division. Set in Berkeley Book Oldstyle. Map by R. R. Donnelley & Sons, Cartographic Services, Lancaster, Pa. Printed and bound by R. R. Donnelley & Sons, Willard, Ohio. Color separations by Graphic Art Service, Inc., Nashville, Tenn.; Lanman Progressive Co., Washington, D.C.; Lincoln Graphics, Inc., Cherry Hill, N.J.; NEC, Inc., Nashville, Tenn.; and Phototype Color Graphics, Pennsauken, N.J. Dust jacket printed by Federated Lithographers-Printers, Inc., Providence, R.I.

ADDITIONAL READING

The reader may wish to consult the *National Geographic Index* for related articles and books. The following books may be of special interest: John Annerino, *Hiking the Grand Canyon;* Bruce Babbitt, *Grand Canyon: An Anthology;* Merrill D. Beale, *Grand Canyon: The Story Behind the Scenery;* Buzz Belknap, *Grand Canyon River Guide;* Alan Berkowitz, *Grand Canyon Trail Guide—North Kaibab;* Stanley S. Beus and Michael Morales (eds.), *Grand Canyon Geology;* William J. Breed, Vern Stefanic, and George H. Billingsley, *Geologic Guide to the Bright Angel Trail;* Bryan T. Brown, Steven W. Carothers, and R. Roy Johnson, *Grand Canyon Birds;* Michael Collier, *An Introduction to Grand Canyon Geology;* C. Gregory Crampton, *Land of Living Rock;* Kim Crumbo, *A River Runner's Guide to the History of the Grand Canyon;* Frederick S. Dellenbaugh, *A Canyon Voyage;* Clarence E. Dutton, *Tertiary History of the Grand Cañon District;* Philip Fradkin, *A River No More;* W. Kenneth Hamblin and Joseph R. Murphy, *Grand Canyon Perspectives;* Rose Houk, *Grand Canyon Trail Guide—South Kaibab;* J. Donald Hughes, *In the House of Stone and Light;* George Wharton James, *In & Around the Grand Canyon;* Michael R. Kelsey, *Hiking and Exploring the Paria River;* Troy L. Péwé, *Colorado River Guidebook;* J. W. Powell, *The Exploration of the Colorado River and Its Canyons;* Connie Rudd, *Grand Canyon—North Rim: The Story Behind the Scenery;* Robert Scharff, *Grand Canyon National Park;* Larry Stevens, *The Colorado River in Grand Canyon;* Stephen Whitney, *A Field Guide to the Grand Canyon.*

*L*ight show commences at sunset at Mather Point, a popular lookout on the South Rim of the Grand Canyon. On the opposite, less visited rim of the gorge, shadows creep across Wotans Throne and Vishnu Temple.

©RIC ERGENBRIGHT

Index

Bold face indicates illustrations.

Library of Congress CIP Data

Fishbein, Seymour L.
    Grand Canyon country / by Seymour L. Fishbein ; prepared by the Book Division. National Geographic Society.
        p.   cm.
    Includes bibliographical references and index.
    ISBN 0-87044-828-5
    1. Grand Canyon National Park (Ariz.) 2. Grand Canyon National Park Region (Ariz.) 3. Fishbein, Seymour L.—Journeys—Arizona—Grand Canyon National Park. I. National Geographic Society (U.S.). Book Division. II. Title.
    F788.F52 1991
    917.91'32—dc20   91-6635
                                                                            CIP

NATIONAL GEOGRAPHIC SOCIETY

"For the increase and diffusion of geographic knowledge."

THE NATIONAL GEOGRAPHIC SOCIETY is chartered in Washington, D. C., as a nonprofit scientific and educational organization. Since 1890 the Society has supported more than 4,000 explorations and research projects, adding to knowledge of earth, sea, and sky.

GILBERT M. GROSVENOR, *President*

Senior Vice Presidents
ALFRED J. HAYRE, *Treasurer and C.F.O.*
JOHN T. HOWARD, *C.O.O.*
MICHELA A. ENGLISH
RAYMOND T. McELLIGOTT, JR.
ROBERT B. SIMS

Vice Presidents
FREDERICK C. GALE, JOSEPH B. HOGAN,
JAMES P. KELLY, ADRIAN L. LOFTIN, JR.,
ROSS L. MULFORD, H. GREGORY PLATTS,
PAUL B. TYLOR
EDWIN W. SNIDER, *Secretary*
SUZANNE DUPRÉ, *Corporate Counsel*

BOARD OF TRUSTEES
GILBERT M. GROSVENOR, *Chairman*
OWEN R. ANDERSON, *Vice Chairman*
LLOYD H. ELLIOTT, *Vice Chairman*
JOE L. ALLBRITTON
Chairman, Riggs National Bank
THOMAS E. BOLGER
Chairman, Executive Committee, Bell Atlantic
FRANK BORMAN
Chairman and CEO, Patlex Corporation
LEWIS M. BRANSCOMB
Kennedy School of Government, Harvard University
ROBERT L. BREEDEN
J. CARTER BROWN
Director, National Gallery of Art
WARREN E. BURGER
Chief Justice of the United States (Ret.)
MARTHA E. CHURCH
President, Hood College
MICHAEL COLLINS
President, Michael Collins Associates
GEORGE M. ELSEY
President Emeritus, American Red Cross
WILLIAM GRAVES
ALFRED J. HAYRE
A. LEON HIGGINBOTHAM, JR., Chief Judge
for the Third Circuit, U. S. Court of Appeals
JOHN JAY ISELIN
President, The Cooper Union
TIMOTHY T. KELLY
J. WILLARD MARRIOTT, JR.
Chairman and President, Marriott Corporation
FLORETTA DUKES McKENZIE
Former Superintendent of Schools, District of Columbia
PATRICK F. NOONAN
President, The Conservation Fund
NATHANIEL P. REED
Businessman-Environmentalist
B. FRANCIS SAUL II
Chairman and CEO, B. F. Saul Company
ROBERT C. SEAMANS, JR.
Department of Aeronautics and Astronautics, MIT

TRUSTEES EMERITUS
CRAWFORD H. GREENEWALT, CARYL P. HASKINS,
MRS. LYNDON B. JOHNSON, WM. McCHESNEY
MARTIN, JR., LAURANCE S. ROCKEFELLER,
FREDERICK G. VOSBURGH, JAMES E. WEBB,
CONRAD L. WIRTH

RESEARCH AND EXPLORATION COMMITTEE
BARRY C. BISHOP, *Chairman;* FRANK C. WHITMORE, JR.,
Vice Chairman; ANTHONY R. DE SOUZA, *Editor,*
National Geographic Research & Exploration; EDWIN W.
SNIDER, *Secretary;* STEVEN S. STETTES, *Asst. Sec.;* H. J. DE BLIJ,
University of Miami; WILLIAM GRAVES; GILBERT M. GROSVENOR;
BETTY J. MEGGERS, Smithsonian Institution; DAVID PIMENTEL,
Cornell University; PETER H. RAVEN, Missouri Botanical Garden;
CHARLES H. SOUTHWICK, University of Colorado;
JOHN H. STEELE, Woods Hole Oceanographic Institution;
GEORGE E. STUART; GEORGE E. WATSON;
RICHARD S. WILLIAMS, JR., U. S. Geological Survey;
HENRY T. WRIGHT, University of Michigan

EDUCATION FOUNDATION
LLOYD H. ELLIOTT, *President;* Betsy Ellison

NATIONAL GEOGRAPHIC MAGAZINE
GILBERT M. GROSVENOR, *President and Chairman*
WILLIAM GRAVES, *Editor*

SENIOR ASSISTANT EDITORS
WILLIAM L. ALLEN, *Pictorial* • ROBERT BOOTH, *Production* • THOMAS Y. CANBY, *Science*
ALLEN CARROLL, *Art* • JOHN B. GARVER, JR., *Cartography* • DAVID JEFFERY, *Legends*
THOMAS R. KENNEDY, *Photography* • ROBERT W. MADDEN, *Layout and Design*
O. LOUIS MAZZATENTA, *Control Center* • ELIZABETH A. MOIZE, *Staff* • ROBERT M. POOLE, *Contract Writers*
JOHN J. PUTMAN, *Manuscripts* • LESLEY B. ROGERS, *Research* • W. ALLAN ROYCE, *Illustrations*
MARY G. SMITH, *Research Grant Projects* • GEORGE E. STUART, *Archaeology* • PRIIT J. VESILIND, *Expeditions*

EDITORIAL
ASSISTANT EDITORS: Judith Brown, William S. Ellis, Rick Gore, Alice J. Hall, Peter Miller, Merle Severy, Peter T. White, Erla Zwingle. SENIOR WRITERS: Thomas J. Abercrombie, Harvey Arden, Mike Edwards, John L. Eliot, Noel Grove, Bryan Hodgson, Michael E. Long. SENIOR EDITORIAL STAFF: Don Belt, Charles E. Cobb, Jr., Boyd Gibbons, Larry Kohl, Douglas B. Lee, Cathy Newman, Cliff Tarpy, Jane Vessels, Margaret N. Walsh, Boris Weintraub. *Production:* John L. McIntosh. EDITORIAL STAFF: Michael Kenna, Thomas O'Neill, Oliver G.A.M. Payne, Peter L. Porteous, A. R. Williams. RESEARCH: Michaeline A. Sweeney, *Assoc. Director; Researcher-Editors:* Carolyn H. Anderson, Ann B. Henry, Jeanne E. Peters. *Researchers:* Danielle M. Beauchamp, Judith F. Bell, Catherine C. Fox, Sheila M. Green, Jan Holderness, Anne A. Jamison, Amy E. Kezerian, Kathy B. Maher, Barbara W. McConnell, Abigail A. Tipton. *Legends:* Victoria C. Ducheneaux, Margaret G. Zackowitz. *Planning Council:* Mary McPeak

ILLUSTRATIONS
PHOTOGRAPHERS: Kent J. Kobersteen, *Assoc. Director;* Susan A. Smith, *Asst. Director;* Joseph H. Bailey, James L. Blair, Victor R. Boswell, Jr., Jodi Cobb, Bruce Dale, Emory Kristof, Joseph D. Lavenburg, George F. Mobley, James L. Stanfield; *Technical:* Claude E. Petrone. ILLUSTRATIONS EDITORS: William T. Douthitt, *Assoc. Director;* David L. Arnold, Dennis R. Dimick, John A. Echave, Bruce A. McElfresh, Charlene Murphy, Larry Nighswander, Robert S. Patton, Elie S. Rogers, Jon Schneeberger, Susan Welchman; Kathy Moran. LAYOUT AND DESIGN: Constance H. Phelps, *Assoc. Director;* Mary Kathryn Glassner, David Griffin; *Typography:* Betty Clayman-DeAtley, Douglas M. McKenney. ART: William H. Bond, Christopher A. Klein, *Artists;* Karen E. Gibbs, *Research.* ENGRAVING AND PRINTING: William W. Smith, *Director;* James R. Whitney, *Assoc. Director;* Judy L. Garvey, Janet C. Novak, Ronald E. Williamson

CARTOGRAPHY
Assoc. Directors: John F. Dorr, Alice T. M. Rechlin, John F. Shupe, Leo B. Zebarth; *Asst. Dirs.:* David P. Beddoe, Harold A. Hanson, Harry D. Kauhane, Richard K. Rogers, Elie Sabban. *Geographer:* Ted Dachtera. *Map Editors:* Charles W. Gotthardt, Jr., *Supvr.;* John T. Blozis, Thomas L. Gray, Etelka K. Horvath, Gus Platis, Jon A. Sayre, Thomas A. Wall, Thomas A. Walsh. *Designers:* John A. Bonner, Robert E. Pratt, Nancy Schweickart, Sally S. Summerall. *Researchers:* John L. Beeson, Dierdre T. Bevington-Attardi, Ross M. Emerson, Marguerite B. Hunsiker, Linda R. Kriete, Gaither G. Kyhos, Mary C. Latham, David B. Miller, Dorothy A. Nicholson, Douglas A. Strobel, Juan J. Valdés, Andrew J. Wahll, Susan Young. *Map Artists:* Roland R. Nichols, *Supvr.;* Iskandar Baday, Edward J. Holland, James E. McClelland, Jr., Stephen P. Wells, Alfred L. Zebarth. *Computer Cartography:* Charles F. Case, Kevin P. Allen, Richard W. Bullington, Arthur J. Cox, Martin J. Golden, Barbara P. Holland, Jonathan E. Kaut, Ellen J. Landsman. *Specialists:* Charles L. Miller, Henri A. Delanghe

EDITORIAL SERVICES
ADMINISTRATION: Benita M. Swash, *Asst. to the Editor;* Elaine Rice Ames, Marie L. Barnes, Barbara D. Case, Sandra M. Dane, Lilian Davidson, Marisa Domeyko, Carol L. Dumont, Neva L. Folk, Eleanor W. Hahne, Ellen E. Kohlberg, Liisa Maurer, Katherine P. McGown, Charlene S. Valeri, Ruth Winston. *Picture Requests:* Barbara A. Shattuck. *Travel:* Virginia A. Bachant, Ann C. Judge. RESOURCES: *Library:* Susan Fifer Canby, *Director;* David C. Beveridge, Arlene T. Drewes, Carolyn Locke, Marta Strada. *Illustrations:* Maura A. Mulvihill, *Director;* L. Fern Dame, Carolyn J. Harrison. *Records:* Mary Anne McMillen, *Director;* Ann E. Hubbs, Mennen M. Smith. *Correspondence:* Joseph M. Blanton, Jr., *Director;* Lee Smith. *Indexes:* Jolene M. Blozis, Anne K. McCain. *Translations:* Kathryn A. Bazo. COMMUNICATIONS: Steve Raymer, *Director, News Service;* Joy Aschenbach, Mercer Cross, Donald J. Frederick, Donald Smith, Robert C. Radcliffe, *Radio.* Dale A. Petroskey, *Asst. Vice Pres., Public Affairs;* Mary Jeanne Jacobsen, Barbara S. Moffet, Susan S. Norton. AUDIOVISUAL: Joanne M. Hess, *Director;* Jon H. Larimore, *Tech. Dir.;* Ronald S. Altemus, Scott A. Brader, Robert G. Fleegal, Paul Gorski, P. Andrew van Duym, Gerald L. Wiley

ADMINISTRATION
ASST. VICE PRESIDENTS: Joyce W. Graves, *Asst. to the President;* Carolyn F. Clewell, Robert G. Corey, Joseph S. Fowler, Donna L. Hasslinger, Thomas E. Kulikosky, Carol E. Lang, Richard A. Mechler, George E. Newstedt, Jimmie D. Pridemore, James G. Schmelzer, Carl M. Shrader, Peter F. Woods. ASST. TREASURER: Dorothy M. Wagner. ASSTS. TO THE PRESIDENT: Richard E. Pearson, *Diplomatic and Civic Affairs;* Karen L. Harshbarger, Karen S. Marsh. ACCOUNTING: Laura L. Leight, Larry E. Dowdy. ADMINISTRATION: M. Jean Vile, *Business Manager;* Mary L. Blanton, Margaret R. Herndon, Robert V. Koenig, Myra A. McLellan, Jennifer Moseley, Joyce S. Sanford, Myla Stewart, Frank M. Twigger, R. Miles White, Janet C. Yates. COMPUTER: Scott Bolden, Warren Burger, William L. Chewning, Curtis L. Conway, Jr., Fred R. Hart, George F. Hubbs, Ronald C. Kline. EDUCATIONAL SERVICES: Wendy G. Rogers, Dean R. Gage. EXPLORERS HALL: Nancy W. Beers, Richard McWalters. GEOGRAPHY EDUCATION DIVISION: Robert E. Dulli, *Director;* Mary Lee Elden, J. Joe Ferguson. HUMAN RESOURCES: Robert E. Howell, Glenn G. Pepperman, Shirley N. Wilson. MEMBERSHIP SERVICES: Barbara M. Davis, Carol A. Houck, Kathleen V. Howard. PROMOTION: Joan Anderson, James V. Bullard, James R. Dimond, Jr., Robert L. Feige, Deborah A. Jones, Charles T. Kneeland, Lucy J. Lowenthal, F. William Rath. PURCHASING: Thomas L. Fletcher, Edmund E. Lapane. FOREIGN EDITIONS: Robert W. Hernandez, *Director*

PRODUCTION SERVICES
QUALITY: Frank S. Oliverio, Bill M. Aldridge. PRE-PRESS: Geoffrey T. McConnell, Martin G. Anderson, Billy R. Barnett, Richard A. Bredeck, David H. Chisman, Phillip E. Plude, Bernard G. Quarrick, John R. Reap. PHOTOGRAPHIC LAB: William S. Petrini, James H. Trott, Alfred M. Yee. PRINTING: Hans H. Wegner, Joseph M. Anderson, Sherrie S. Harrison. ADMINISTRATION: Lawrence F. Ludwig, *Director;* Joan S. Simms

ADVERTISING
Joan McCraw, *Vice President and Director;* Debra J. Grady, *New York Manager;* O. W. Jones, Jr., *Detroit Manager;* James D. Shepherd, *Western Manager;* Philip G. Reynolds, *Special Accounts Manager;* Laurie L. Kutsche, *Chicago Manager;* Michel A. Boutin, *International Director,* 90, Champs-Élysées, 75008 Paris; Bernadette Lorda, *International Manager,* New York. Washington: Alex MacRae, *Marketing/Sales Development;* Pandora B. Todd, *Promotion;* Sarita L. Moffat, *Operations;* Renee S. Clepper, *Research;* Gail M. Jackson, *Production*

TELEVISION
Timothy T. Kelly, *Vice President and Director;* Tom Simon, *Co-Executive Producer;* Julia Mair, *Programming;* Susan Borke, *Business Operations;* Todd Berman, *Marketing;* Kathleen F. Teter, *Public Relations;* Patricia Gang, *Film Library;* Yeorgos N. Lampathakis, Marjorie M. Moomey, Nola L. Shrewsberry. EDUCATIONAL FILMS: Sidney Platt, *Director;* Donald M. Cooper, *Assoc. Dir.;* Suzanne K. Poole, Carl E. Ziebe

EDUCATIONAL SERVICES OF THE SOCIETY
ROBERT L. BREEDEN, *Executive Adviser to the President*
Donald J. Crump, *International Publications;* Stephen J. Hubbard, Carolyn W. Jones. BOOK DIVISION: William R. Gray, *Asst. Vice President and Director;* Margery G. Dunn, *Senior Editor;* John G. Agnone, Greta Arnold, Leah Bendavid-Val, Jody Bolt, Jane H. Buxton, Victoria Cooper, Richard M. Crum, Mary Dickinson, Suzanne C. Eckert, Karen F. Edwards, Toni Eugene, Ron Fisher, Patricia F. Frakes, Victoria D. Garrett, Mary Ann Harrell, Carolinda E. Hill, Suez B. Kehl, Ann N. Kelsall, Charles Kogod, Marianne R. Koszorus, Artemis S. Lampathakis, J. Edward Lanouette, Bonnie S. Lawrence, Rebecca Lescaze, Sandra F. Lotterman, Tom Melham, H. Robert Morrison, Elizabeth Newhouse, Melanie Patt-Corner, Barbara A. Payne, Thomas B. Powell III, Cynthia Ramsay, Cinda Rose, Margaret Sedeen, Gene S. Stuart, Penelope Timbers, Jennifer C. Urquhart, Richard Wain, Marilyn Williams. MAGAZINE DIVISION: David P. Johnson, *Director;* Douglas E. Hill, *Financial Director; Traveler:* Richard Busch, *Editor;* Paul Martin, *Managing Editor;* Lyle Rosbotham, *Art Dir.; World:* Pat Robbins, *Editor;* Susan M. Tejada, *Managing Editor;* Ursula Vosseler, *Art Dir.;* Charles E. Herron, *Senior Illustrations Editor.* EDUCATIONAL MEDIA: George A. Peterson, *Asst. Vice President and Director;* Jimmie Abercrombie, Julie V. Agnone, David Beacom, Rick Bounds, Monica P. Bradsher, James B. Caffrey, Carolyn Hatt, James Hiscott, Jr., Turner Houston, Betty G. Kotcher, Louise C. Millikan, Lise Olney, Linda Rinkinen, Barbara Seeber. PUBLICATIONS ART: John D. Garst, Jr., *Director;* Virginia L. Baza, *Assoc. Dir.;* Peter J. Balch, Gary M. Johnson. MANUFACTURING: George V. White, *Director;* John T. Dunn, *Assoc. Dir.;* Robert Messer, Gregory Storer